THE WHITE MUSEUM

THE WHITE MUSEUM

L y n n e   D r e y e r

ROOF

Some of these pieces were originally published as chapbooks or in small press magazines: *Lamplights Used to Feed the Deer* by Some of Us Press; *Stampede* by E.E.L. Press; *The Letters* in *Tottel's;* and *Tamoka* in *ROOF.* In addition, parts of this book were previously published in: *L=A=N=G=U=A=G=E, The Big House, None of the Above, Washington Review of the Arts, The Paris Review, Vanishing Cab, Mass Transit, Dog City,* and *boundary 2.*

Front cover painting by Miriam Laufer. *Tondo,* 1965. Oil on masonite, diameter 40 inches.

ISBN: 0–937804–21–5

Library of Congress Catalog Card Number: 86–061580

This publication is funded in part by a grant from the National Endowment for the Arts.

ROOF BOOKS
are published by
The Segue Foundation
300 Bowery
New York, NY 10012

THE WHITE MUSEUM

Stampede

As in the word, air rises singular motions, ears replacing them to invite their own to mine. As if we were limited in supplies, he stands on sand dripping. As if families had meant more, generosity, meeting, playing games early before she had married your father or younger boys.

Clear eyes—who thought of bearness and business in complete succession, when he looked older he looked handsome, he looked, could never hunger for here and in the city—free. He thought the logs were fake. He was finished with machines. He thought it was personal and he might not get in. From schools he kept counting, didn't repel candies from the South. and commented on everyone's work. Ruptured skin—the only vibrant words.

Would I have been born out of nought? They were always changing—thrash rocks where you found your emptiness—where you found routine. Snakes switch eyelids forming small cuts, they made the word capillary, they knew it meant road.

When all else seemed to stop—magnets formed bridges going. Skulls vibrated sounds in which my heart beat that you ignored, practiced to hear. She sang in silence—turns speaks and breathes in bodies, her way of becoming sophisticated. Yet sleeves tore and words were always unintelligible, it was a rush written. It was his cry. She always changed—even to the extremes of accents. Other people have called it a surrender, a type of act or misplaced book. Still it took time, still every stitch rich with laughter, excitement, copies, one who came in took pictures, filled up space, or fitted space. Were you wanting things or thinking that they could bring you other things?

It's a poem, they're all nurses.
It's a poem—he comments on other women, ones in which notes were taken back, described read in various accents. It was the voice. Did she take coats, ones that aimed, ones that made her famous, ones that made her tough. Given—luck and shorter laughter—waiting.
He said you need thread.
He was embarrassed.
It showed her neck.
It was a different girl. It separated sound. It formed couples, stations that were cold, were not the modern ones, were heavy with screeching monologues or looks or waiting.

Elephants wait too slowly—in a stampede they wait, fly from trains, car to car thinking. If I was loose, I would understand accents and public places, and the ability of calming gestures. Ribs crushed as they passed through. Infrequent sounds starved for laughter or noise or wanting to stop for music boxes.

It might have been the wrong car, or her need to stare out of the kitchen window to a cement block wall. It might have been that nothing was there. The day we made food he would jump. The day we made food we were too comfortable or clean and the ability to make the jump seemed no less real only farther. Space formed between jumps. If I ran I would wear a ring loosely fitted, take later trains to see her. Fish provided stories but I never heard her voice exaggerated that way for children.
Lustage Welt—Happy Wood.
Mira—why do they all sit so blindly and read as if their antagonism was to be in exactly that aisle or window. She invited him to look at

the view. She wants him to travel down with her. They sleep she falls with envy.

He sounded like copy. Stampede—when certain animals rush too slowly, jungle thrush, fragrant moments. Diamonds cut, form slowly into ice, into practical things. Rings Marriage Pearls their clearness, where water was not with general fish but specific works. And how I had been through all that. Their call. They rush more swiftly now, rush harder blocks on blocks building them falling each one separately changing each as if they were actually listening to the voice. In the island grotesque faces form out from the sea, hand on branches waiting to be picked. Ripe crops not yet ready for other fields.

Three forms walk in Antarctica. He spoke of the North Pole. Blood spots on snow which I jumped through knowing it was only there I was safe or the fact that with each stampede wind flew into my face not bruising or biting but softening certain features into one complete mass.

He had no nose. He had a bandage. He was shielded, waited for times when everyone wouldn't ask when? Why does it matter how I breathe? Plants can do it without the change of voice-closed. She finds voyage—she runs. Plants are killed by Tchaikovsky's music. They may use information to make food, to make them more comfortable. To give him courage to make introductions without names.

Pens held pens when his job seemed only to slice boxes, sit them large enough and slice them again. He is still. He is running. He is keeping his word, not in the honest sense. He seems to be making things. Was the fact that eyes—coffee—that without. Was friendship that close or the fact that we both missed points. Her hand always on the hollow of her neck. Or hallways. She does each separate.

Singular motions droop in the sun urging them to come up,

stop and fall making the ground more fertile for children. The fact is they don't care. The fact that they're always running making their own. They want to share, wear clothes, think up ideas and follow each one through. Had she held the Gothic Arch and fitted cylinders into it? Had she handled each one carefully or marked the prices down and ran pushing through to the shore and blocked the voice out? As if seeing was hearing, when one is absent the other stronger more absolute.

The result was a lobotomy or going out to dinner. They go to the zoo, this time caged in. It seemed they made babies. It always seemed to work. The essence was not grammar. The essence was that he who raises his voice sees all of them. Hooded men were priests. Must be his Irishness. Must be his kingdom or need to be the best. Four flowers fall patiently in his brain. Bring the food waking dry with laughter. I heard her voice before I met her. I had her voice. I knew how to go on accepting the wind, always in my face, again masses. Stampede masses.

Stampedes, schools where they called poetry his life, children his life caresses his life, everything they called it negated his life, built men from other men. Unintelligible matters heard from crevices. Was it more common in winter? Was it the wind, determination or patience?

In Rockland they swim in thorazine when the lights go out to make it easier on them. Neighbors wait with rifles ready for the stampede yet still I hold her clenched fists wanting. Your cheeks already more swollen than mine.

Concentration on laughter and his stinginess about his paper. I could write take flight anywhere. Yet when I lived there I was one, carrying cases fitted with smaller men and voices. Trains, parts of men, and their modern decor, their intention to wishful thinking. I think of summer and not stampedes.

At the flick of a switch all mood changes, gifts are accepted, pictures conversed in detail, trips taken, tea is tenser and placed on the shelf. On Wednesdays it is simpler. On Wednesdays it is always done. Had he arranged his death or other funerals or looked the pigs death in the face? Had he become religious? With rain and grounded rabbits. What is here and the North Pole and things always happen but on Wednesdays it is different. They come wanting ideas.

I carry branches.

Your image of weakness.
My knowledge of strength. She is lost knows much. It is not from her mother or families or origins and seeking them out. Becoming more with houses. This is why everything is new in houses and keeping them clean. This she said was discipline. The words caught in her throat. Had she become past tense? Here points become valises. Facts hieroglyphics. Muted lights non-distinct voice what to take. It seemed long. I remember pictures and copies of words on them. Specific rubies without their directness. His laughter was wishful. His laughter was killed and made into different parts of bodies. Amputations and what they did with them. It seemed they did it to music. The next memory was medical. Schooling and teaching. Saying much to each other, slicing boxes, bodies withheld.

As if they knew the word day.
As if they knew songs without words and came across these songs in morgues. Not their teaching, not pictures, not smaller attempts but symbols of parts, put away.

They carried them downstairs, babies that would explode, go to clubs and dance even at that age. Stamps made, pictures in which singular drips rambled throughout foresought much laughter and tried to understand their generosity of taking. Pools Chinese torture step up step up. All of us. One of us. Logs as if were water. They were rifles. Consciously debris as if we were ceasing or only words. It was a comedy. Camps where concentration ceased and routine was only necessary. Her attire was a tank. In flippers one with shoes that showed her stroke. I had let cleanliness kill the symbol a rifle—a pool.

Mark II A pen.

He started small as in smaller cities, as humility took every inch of his body. At five the city starts profit, resume, we take each others parts and hold fast, figuring the differences of skins, of pressures, of minutes, of cooking. As in the word light her costume beckoning all of smaller ones and filled bags with candy and shells. They dressed alike, their difference was attachment to each other and books saying how they were alike unpleasant but not unpleasant to speak of in circuses.

They dressed for fun, ran to other parts of the world, beckoning their subjects. He writes letters, shredded lines. He repeats waits for the same when actuality crept, fluorescent witnesses crept, science crept, lameness slivering each hold.

Did you see the snake?

They're riding. Every epidermi favorite flavors—ones that were stores. You could travel through pick out what you thought.

Picked cold. Were or how we just "made it on time and how just making it"

It-trees rode ran into smaller fields ran through lines, if I was there.

Bridges form inconsistent memories, spots where you held yourself, cooled down, laughter continued running. His nose grows back. Perfect lines where pens were held, Matrix, boxed in walls, where she sat. That we may help you remember your name. Comes from watching your singular apparel each scarf carefully draped. It is here in the line. It is my father. I hold her. I think she's long. I hold her.

Skin thwarted, lobster crush their sides, here he is serious and can know his sides, violence joking, and his job. Unlatched letters waited the openings. Would paper replace voice or the matrix of the voice? Would paper replace the loss of voice.

With nylons the entire style changed, forcing ideas into sounds or trying to leave them out. Sweat wipes each linoleum tile into favorite things and songs. I buy a song and look at rings yet when I look at him trusting him again rushes pawn to king to have power. She can move. He has power. She jumps pawn forces
openings
on mandolins or maudlins, leave her drink unfinished, lives her life orally, lives openings, and can walk masses, walk each bridge closer or walking into structures completed.

And movies where they stood out, made them thinner and talked about her. I hold her voice and am given a tour. She wears spiders another one relaxes laps up snakes, lady flips, knows tunes and gives up miseries.
Houses sheets promises. Restless go planetariums, think light shows. I go on trips thinking that one I'll stop. Pharmeceutical animals become boring, numbering each scratch and crevice in her skin. She calls not that it was old times but that it was there. What do these hands do? Kill and all gentleness. Kill and refractioned glances.

Knowing his violence. Men who live men. Kiss my hand twice in a week that boys picked calves, wore army boots and still alert and is still walking. Aretha becomes skinny, shapelier in her act doesn't seek respect, but invites unopened letters throbbing with want.

Wanting shows.
Wanting good-byes.
Wanting to stop without.
When I speak each sound freezes my tongue.
His understanding of void and wanting it. And comfort and life with that. He made the men in cages even laugh. Technical aides that her mother was taught, was dead, and kept burnt paper.

Was it only in basements where the poets kept it separate, holy even to the word? Is she still out there walking each field, as she expected strange-lit gardens to teach her botany. If it resembles store windows it may be real. Auras are created by electrons coinciding with nitrogen atoms. They tried to imagine what many lands had. Our black man on top of the world, The subject begins, change channels, begin writing or saying his life. Cabin boys sailed to China followed trips. Music increases as ash and they have sounds to discover, It is cold. He learned their ways and lines and sets with frozen eat.

I reach out for stringed light, walls which were sterile, which made them rush to eat. When he was three he ran, bridges formed under his pounce, leaving, reinforcing each step.
Effort increased with every step.

Name, busy, closed. Part particles with structure, feel peculiarities of intake, seek formulas that wrestle with voices. Polished each leaf with conversation. He taught himself, he knew how to read. This is the part where he picks up one. This he says out loud. His hunger is to solve formulas ceased in three seconds. Cracks lamented songs, where not as held small instruments, was wearing an effect held, or held objects. Ones where strangers seemed only necessary to warrant her life complete, not meaning history of books or animals. The history of each act. Every move a brink, a decision withheld. Wounds where only animals dared to eat, to gorge on his particles or meet at the station to pick up trains. Kids play on metal thinking there toys, their toys. Culture Bus loops. Tapestries—Rivers.

Where she wrote from, where she stepped with stones, rivers where she severed their eyes, pressures of lobotomies of a poem without. I laugh ash to the wind. Mannequins dress themselves under the spell of some sordid fuel. They show her with two faces. I drop my voice in the dirt. Step on it viciously and let it grow. They notice seasons as if they were always changing, in one room they change clothes without the use of biographies. They were a group.

They tampered with things religiously. In services, in every walk, still fresh with leisure or going home.

Lights, fragmented songs.
Small instruments hang from his car and ear.
Pictures wait maternally.
Museums—white nights.
Museums statues.

Given—when water finds. If I was down there looking. Rocks are one part of the body organ. Organs are one part. At six there is dinner in which each dress galloped through. He says she has a head. He is joking. Each organ—separate classes, she would teach one. She would sever her eyes before she knew of novocaine, walk to the sea to rock. He inhaled the stones, dresses entered before they were announced and were numerous. Her clothes were necessary and not planned.

Before she had lived off of the floor in every possible way she explained items to their last detail. Detail composed. Without wanting them. Machines and how they seemed to go on working when buttons were pressed to stop, when pills were pressed to stop, stop stiffness, stop exploring. Older women offered to buy her beds. Parts of the body are placed on the dresser. Plastic arms which cried, which moved even in their own limbs.

Blood water they laugh. Thrash voice. If they're changing style, they're changing voice. Smart the scale weighed in the correct lines jewelry. Most of it is junk.
Some of it is smarter. Boats that wear.
Lily white she paints traces in magnets faces drawn toward them.

They held back they wait. Freshly made scores from laps. Lap water lap milk to speak to look each other in the eye. She wears black, she is stronger. Wares buys her wares makes coffee, makes pain. The day it was made we were late. The day it was made we were tied to exact language and recipes.

Think twice thrice think twice to jump. When I'm helpful I'm more interesting. I give up one. I give up. I give up one I give up.

Bright eyes are synonymous with modest warfare. They shot them killing hundreds at one time. I'm in a pool sucking bullets leaving holes, I'm still breathing in more, stones slide, step up and walk, sort them out loud, study them. Eruption and study fit together in exactness, in walking, almost properness. In almost walking.

In the garden she had no children. In the garden she was a man and free.

He knows something He is standing alone borrowing pens that are thrown from outer hands. Radiant dreams. If he found a fawn he ran. Lily white masterpiece. Lily white her master.
Do one more.
Do one more.

I couldn't work, heard my father shrink from comfort, from concerts, from luxury with warm channels. He changes them. He wanted change.

Modest warfare. I heard once it was sixty. I can't hide behind that machine.

Cruelty to horses, Black Beauty. She travelled to machines, returning to her name. Modest warfare it's over. Worried looks compare movies to the law. If he's coming it's time, it's cleared out.

Was it a memorial? In Stockholm everyone was light. She had small incomes and couldn't accept smells thinking them not inhuman. I heard knocks. I'm concentrating, found my chart was ruled by the sun, the moon, or fire. On fire it's hidden, on fire, blackness comes back in forms of hooded men, chisels, moving in, seeing, and knowing which was hidden and which was a man. I reach inside of me.

At that point everything became more precious. Women sell cat pictures on the street. I am born. Teaching the atrocities of bodies and touch, I walk step by step. My hands where they leave you where blackness as that much stronger where silence held notes.
I trust two of you.
I trust two, remember money and fill applications learn more of the swelling and forget its meaning. He is silent after talk of strangers. He is my father. Where do rooms meet? In the center where they are hollow. Where the books lay in neat piles touched by individual fingers and one.
He's a king.
He's a book.
He's the king. He remembered his voice where he found it. Blatant figures pour out from the sun.

He's the king. He sits by the corner, the queen's tea set has broken under his pensive stare. She has the right to say it. Kings on bags. Oil draped.
I want a jar.
I want you.
I want a jar.
I want you.
Not poetic inquiries, not drama.
Matriarchal figures faded into pleasant memories. No death here except memory. And judgement. Bridal costumes. I hide under a fence, dogs, and moments. Flush that she risked her life. Flush that he was an aristocrat. Flush that he was jealous and still. To record a

baptism the child was smarter, hung from flagpoles, and saluted. Scream in the middle, rides, take time.
Musicians and the Power of Walruses
or that I am with a Greek completely alone touching beds, taming them into original writing. They know you mostly speak. They speak mostly.
nothing from seeds.
Almost up to techniques, I rush songs that were stolen and clarified independent of each other. She swallowed or how one could sit and drink words so as to allow a certain space between them, a silence as in action watching them I began to feel my voice had nothing to do with anyone, each antennae was an apology, classed and boxed. I decided not to speak into that peril and danger.

The beat how it could save a life. He was serious played each note. Meeting we climb flagpoles and hang limply. Angular faces looked up to the effect into romantic language. It was the word that made them climb.

There—where science made them realize biographies and the tragedy of his optimistic outlook on life. Everyone saluted, slash them meaning correct names and places cleaning toms where they hung pastel clothes. It was soon spring, they would try to wear them then. She carried her time in small change, didn't request things or that they charged each face without knowing detail.

Understanding his crime he gave a talisman and direct language. It was not a report. It was Hungarian. How trees formed for authors, certain people or details. It seemed whimsical, not dramatic but like a certain dress which captivated numbers and pens held up, or how things can blatantly change saying general things.

Living in rooms not houses seen cameras relinquish their oneness. Adding musicians to each note. How do you ask the price of apples? That was said to be free. Body-individual artillery.

To invite intake to want wait patiently this after stampedes after snakes had rushed their heads into the ground their bodies. In the rush, their bodies awakened gracefully nodding blood.
Stampede Panic Pan.
Sudden hushes limited Pan. Here he felt and learned three things.

1. Beating on tables to break them
2. Beating with two fingers
3. How to write words so others could read them.

He took medication sometimes hiding it under his tongue, sometimes spitting it on his shirt. Let us just put the seeds on top of them and let them grow. Let us show books our nakedness. Let us cry and hang the faces from their picks. Pick laughter which tried to encourage more potent medicine. He cut glass. He cut his hand carried scars became gentle and went outside, learned to use time for dialogue and wood.
Specialists.
Dialogues with disease and how they classified. him. He drew water and soaked with her waiting, dropping his body and clothes.

He remembered fighting, rushes where it didn't go, where it went cutting glass, fractioned forms relatives how they always seemed to transplant non-care to care and houses. When I wore the room I'm cold, can stay in one place not moving.

Learn the value of things, and hands touching hands. Had they formed bodies into work and took trips to wake them into disguises. Had they allowed the country into their bones.
Foreign enemies surrounded their territory.
I rush cold.
I rush talk and want you that way. Hand turning mine to heated skin.

Cooling we wrestle falling from the tips of mountains air.

Here the fight becomes harder.
Sweat pours reluctantly ignoring the others.
I hear the way you eat.
Not thinking transplants
Not thinking trips
Not thinking discharges and know the moment.
Home is blending.
Rooms where they learned from them.
That they would have stopped for children. Here they saw frogs and the rocks became slippery. Mothers would have done the same. The same had been done. Not flowers, not bank accounts but walks where they slashed oranges warning their sweetness, warning their presence.

He entered the basement. It was time wrestled with laughter thorazine and important writing.

All through care, they stopped to care imagined relatives leaving their bones to be picked and moved into one casket.

Together in death they realized their emptiness their primal want to be closed to close. I carry food at that time in the month to encompass everything.

Pictures ones that included fruit and famous men. When I'm around them I'm thwarted. Sand Dunes Women Dunes Men captured. If physical poetry is our likeness we should wear larger sizes not inhale. Boxed floors empty and here I write.

Universities where babies are kept clean to make malteds to make them fatter. She was glowing. He had piles of colors on the floor.

Beds sit welcome time to encourage. I laugh ash, this time to move violent friends.

In some rooms they were occupied with rash and settled lava. They had expected to send him there. Ala saga goola gunno achee gooma lakachee sals chee oola papa chee which stay from morning. Eventually we will all drown swallowing necessary elements from the earth. These include doctors and encouragable laughter from the sun.

Self-portrait. Stainless flatware that is graceful. Now is the moment I hear you. In the state don't let anyone sigh. She walked with many arms around her. The space between fingers disappeared. Calling hours ideas, I see heat rise with satisfaction to the extreme point.
Rain or thunder telling various members of the tribe advice. They were Cherokee, they listened to what they made.

When I look at viewpoint it is optimistic, yet what I feel is a ghostlike existence and weak. People are satisfied with brushing against each other shadow to shadow. and what I need is to enter into something
that completely involves me.

If my voice is failing me I will wear black, change the voice gradually or stop talking. I must learn to enjoy being alone again being free of my own thoughts and get or not want that involvement. Not lose and need so much of self. Dedication to something or someone. Riding across the desert, effort, release, pain, appearance, shelter, non-shelter. The beat how it could sustain a life. With countries musicians cowboys always coming. We lived where the walls were shaped into formidable colors and quite fashionable in that day. In that day her ways were waves. She fell realizing that get was not an act but a receptive voice. Daily activities became her existence. The choice of three things.
1. screaming
2. learning to scream
3. learning her strength. She grew falling from exhaustion. No room

became her own. Pain was that which made her empty to receive.

Fixed relations managed themselves. There was no room on the boat for families. Laps of water continued yet not one drop was wet. Shielding their touch fingers grasped out for hands. Ruins that were torn and rashed.

Here where water reached gut. Where joined knowledge of mermaids increased. He realized his next action. Four eyes. Tired of methodic medicine relentlessly dripping from the exact center of his head titles formed.

Invite bikes or theft from patients. Did they need the song? I carry ferries and strike small poses. Choice of staying or leaving or figuring if women should be assistants or not. If they are they should practice and learn work if they are their clothes should fit. She's too serious and poses as the wife takes rent and becomes the rent and becomes as the rest of the species.

Profound species are ignoring our walks. At four in the city we leave and take smaller rides to smaller cities. In his other life he was a cockroach and fell in love with Cleopatra. This was one she could not accept.

He's editing his music and is keeping clean. The rest of the species are taking clean walks, each step direct from their capillaries. She's encompassed everything during that time of the month, or felt the need to get it all.

If there is losing his pureness money comes in from the disabled patients. They are getting out. They are waiting before, becoming their dinner and the stone was unveiled. In other countries they are buried directly in the ground without the use of caskets.

The flag was in between the letter n and p. yet still he seemed to take her as serious, trying, making fun from seaweed. She made cakes instead. Titles of books fall through my eyes. All of those days were a dream hidden and sometimes mentioned. Confined time and how it meant to be free. The room contained everything, dolls, flags, caloric composition, a telescope, two desks, books, and other things from childhood.

I see my father's pictures in windows. Quietly pack the dogs, fitted mules for muted laughter.

Deciding to walk, I encompass everything on the block from Blake to chips of jazz. Yet still the map of the world hung in the corner of my room. Poetry from friends and still not understood. Poetic stamps are stifling my hold.

We make cards realizing that this would not be the last time, only a week of fasting would be necessary. I began to develop a strong kinship towards philosophical cockroaches and cats, knew the counselor read the same books but in a lighter vein. If that song's on — he's on for the moment reading other girls' hands.

Swallow it. It was a normal day, quite contrary to the rest. Everyone kept calling from all over the country and wanting to know reasons. She leaves silence not knowing her power to stay or say or aggression reaps every ten seconds on the speedometer or pulls back. When the stomach is filled and that is why people are fat or are forever moving their mouths.

They are working on programs or baking cakes. Beauticians have retired and there is a pound cake, a wallet, and some hidden ice-cream. Inside of the punch are oranges, all of the things that I'm accustomed to eating. He couldn't see me dressed yet chocolate is better, but when I think of him it's only a point of cold hands on hot skin and how the two form sweetly together in one large vat. The vat was one separate part of my life.

Mumbles from Seton. Don't come downstairs A touch with. Penny

I'm losing much. I'm losing much. I'm losing much with Penny. In barred regimes I heard tapes the introduction of the great her voice more formal and French.

Explain intake to the reason wind, smaller windows where he held Blake in his hands. This is the game of planting and reaping of the letter A. Hospital socks held a certain way on feet, the beginning of her energy without. Phones, Indian necklaces held the lamp. They lingered on with a certain smell. One cousin was a tyrant. He spilled his cactus on the floor.

I clean out the brush erase hair to forget, hating the color pink using it. One at the windows comes two, I change gather sticks making stories other tales to tell.

I press tombstones together, mashing the bodies, dig out bones, eat the marrow. Everyone's crying, everyone's crying. I skip off to pick flowers. They remain with their families huddled to block wind. To block wind is to block the body. I press hands together callousing the side of my hand. or making it hard in other ways he taught me.

In other ways he taught me tapes, editing. In other ways he thought that moments and taught me those. I carry pages leafing various aspects of my past. Dramatic interior of the door and lies. They were ultimately helping. Scenic views corresponding to foot. When I began to believe he carried the cross, Porcha got out separately, being sent to programs that they built. In each occasion a circle was drawn.

He huddled small instruments, in valises, sometimes bringing them out enclosing them to his chest. In these sounds Indian words in their receptiveness left open for wounds. He sat down, resounding biographies of the word he knew. He woke up with it, took cold showers to slash it from his brain, to remember it, to coincide it with his life.

Adam and Eve went to the bar, waiting for dinner waiting for the word yet knowing it was time for therapy. Are they allowed in small states. I would help him, telling him to bring into his body all the words that he could, for the next few days he would carry nothing. Nothing to which artists would draw their faces muddled with fat with conversation.
Is it dusty?
It's not love.
Is it dusty?
It's just one more day. feeling bars when he jumped he was a salesman selling his wares to strangers, or a marine settling in a different port becoming accustomed to their way of life.

Back in the city, Dalmane to 1. Back in the city to move to friends. Mutters, insipient whines, dancing to fences. I would hear him say. Sometimes you lose friends that way. His forehead showed. Supposed chances. Light life from letters. She would argue his breakfast hoping his slacks were the right size.

Porcha is getting out, being sent to programs that they built. June was that to believe. Hieromagnonomous—wake of the word and forget it make long calls to chickens. In each occasion a circle was drawn, relaxed to very diameters. Your supposed changes, or how she felt letters to be important and not sex. or a rock and relaxed.

Save beach notes, stamps and God's eyes. Bro—when I'm with him, his mother putting him up in hotels and fighting for non-military reasons. An inch of madness crept in. Freedom remained. The drawer was filled.
He kept his things under wood, in thistles, yet they were still after

him believing the knife. He let go of the knife, of his friends and stole knives thinking I've been with women of all sizes yet still she's oppressed by her size. still encompassing everything from ideas to food, or cartoon caricatures of ones she loved.
I see that far in June. The anniversary of the wedding. It is night. What books leave on top.

The White Museum

To Phyllis Rosenzweig

Vague in the morning's light. Shapes cradled into latent hues, psychic tension posed. In the office, three walls making it seem staged. It had nothing to do with her life. Schizophrenic writing examining it counting to eight.

This is the heap. Will the characters follow? You still look like yourself though no more research is done for the contenders weight. How many people have found that the singular hand can not hold you.

The short moment becomes your home. Are you having someone else's dream, talking to them, comforting them so that the boy symbol becomes the poem? Tiny images flash past. A voice paying for your choice. Liquid mouths dream blood, boat capsized heading south. Spread out everything in front of you and think of this as gauze, security as something you actually hold. Sympathy into a murky grin. The impossible structure crippling your gaze. The eyes are charged around the heart and some of the more innocent ones are mistaken for some of the vicious ones and left permanently still. It happens on the most ordinary days. You are taken in and you know it. Hand on mouth, fingers apart, you give everything a name. The night becomes the century's end. Gradually light splits and on that night we name other as sentiment is gathered from the long moon.

I was transporting my own for there were no more gray translations, where the victims were women and wanting it that way. It was a professional error. Like a long dull gray light am I left with my mother's disease.

Honey napkins, blond pageboy and two boys mesmerized by a perfumed card. I read two lost facts and someone said, "All theories are lost." Empty hands gather in all the voices. Rest, conceal, becomes a tiny point of light.

Cow's eyes staring—aviation style. A picture of a window with stars painted on it. Look into the light and picture this. For when you are silent you become open. A bunch of Freudian houses burning, reappearing as if time meant the dreams desire, what comes out of the dream? They learn to use their hands as eyes. They are not acting. Hindrances, mind lackluster, brain fused. Artist to child back to friend carried to the museum or shelf. Enjoy the physical dream. Free the style, practice, question. Cat's eyes swimming, Anacostia, a sense of returning, of going back, of escape, keeping watch. You whites all look the same. The melancholy posture of people visiting a ship was forming. The time was forming and all the time there was the constant trend of being chased. A rape of shoes with a woman on the floor. This was advertising, pointed boots. Could you feel the roof was falling down, the growing out of the yard. It will be a good yard when they are older. An entire baseball field. He was looking at me but couldn't see me. He looked like he had given up but didn't understand.

Explain, meena, class reaction, paying for quiet. Quaint becomes a desert meaning and I become an alien, titles, uniform and character posing talking.

White and tense plastic pigs stand at complete attention. Hover and quiet, night spreads ancient derogatory words.

Why do you follow when there is so little left to do? I'm left feeling empty as a predicted dream.

For the fantasy becomes the victim's hearty laugh. They slip in and out of poses, head on neck, family portraits, old fashioned clothes. Lighting, nocturnal pressure of coming home. Your victim embraces you, perched feet, awaiting praise.

Luminous and studied, the carriage filled with a pile of wood. Survivors who hold no grudge, a baby with a piece of wood thru its head. The modern heart wraps a loop around the future. Books warped against the wind.

We are each separate people. Sticks on the green waiting for the large hand to direct you or hold you up. Marpled books on the water. Watching them go. Sky becoming an indirect voice waiting for veils.

Adjacent, meandering, like a bunch of worried heroes flocking towards each other after the war. For those who come quietly are crowded with abstract thoughts, the sun dropping out of the sky, the hand at noon.

Are phrases not enough? Do I need pictures of nature, clear instead of a pile lapse into solitary view, comfort in the knife, the cup letting the only gutteral sound to form in some strange German dialect.

Simple words let the sky bring some other light not of dawn but early evening light. It was vague like someone's lost impression—the clouds, the sky.

Constant reminder light prisms bring in the house. These carry you into the night interrupting the sound of your voice.

There is a quieting down. It was a mistake. There is no internal you. After all is said picture equalling some other suggests some ultimate decision. The questions are old like sun laced in an old house. Next you read the moon the bread—silly to find somewhere to eat because.

The Americans are posing as Europeans and the Europeans are posing as South American and the South American poses as Chinese. The ringmaster looked Chinese. Let the time dissolve into something fluid where you can't really think. The symbols take on the meaning do.

I didn't hear an original word. This becomes exhausting to the voice. What sounds are here creating an earthy radiant presence of light for when you laugh at these characters you become a kind of goon. Writing slips away and you become small.

Shimmering deer hang onto the trees spread out like a capital C howling in the minted light. A band of little boys waiting on the unhappy pavement trying to find home.

The white hour becomes light fractured into some relentless hero. Things are timed taken not in a whim counted measured played out. Each of the women are writing of the war repeated to the end, repeated towards the end.

The shooting fountain, an overseer protected by gauze, a victim reporting its wounds, peculiar and transient, wistful and loving.

He gives an order then reminisces about wanting to burn his father's house down. Do you follow the words, sit in the ancient playground, dream of electric fires, solo in the eccentric hound.

The blue becomes an exit to the city alphabet, county letters. For in your posture are you only alone. Arms on side, head perched and the gentle repetitious studying of the hands. Noise gradually becomes more distant, a truck becomes a tarnished drink. The long low room is a huge eye. Steps not imagined, but imagine all of the oceans, the cities layed out in some extraordinary way victims everywhere, children hiding, monkey growing into apes, T.V.'s lined up on the beach, the harbor city cracked from the sun. Do you imagine a cow as a wife? An only instrument is. Watching all of these cowboys we do feel and the humility and caution of the scientist is only an excuse. They speak to carry each others voices reminiscent of the journey home. Waving in fluid gestures, the slow return, words pressed on their heads. A lot of soldiers in my neighborhood after the war and all of your white cattle sent out to graze. The cobra is in the tub. Layers of heart, are clustered. The heart pushed towards home.

Language machines are finally at rest, translucent in their form. The wet night rests pressing ancient words independent of their meaning. Barricades against its savage self. Tiny fingers crawl into your skin, vacuous eyes repeating their comic vowels.

Charged out of mind. A fine point in old air. Eyes appear without faces, focusing on the final dream. Admitting some remembered act as the old war passes through our sons kicking them into battle posture voices intact. Hiroshima through Virginia's memory for no one will remember asking wit to be compared to tragedy (at the base) pictures covered heads erect.

The creak begins a tiny well, lazy and slow wave written as a pictorial wave turned dry opening to pink.

A patterned tragedy, a necessary dream. Bags of furniture lay devastated by the long flat version of life. The eyes are opened, accepting memory, some emotional wish nagging at the heart. Stepping into real space muted by time wanting to make secure some deed, typography lacking mean; "epic with no god."

Small things stated frequently. Casually resisting her mother's arms, the last attempt at storytelling becomes comical almost brief and small gestures become stereotypical of the wind. For here we are damaged by the wind at the neck pulling dead weight, a glued on phrase of its own.

A battered correspondence, the second sun violating the sky. Voices call out to each other through the dry wall of the wind, erasing the sawed off moon. They become a test of acquired accents between the thinking and unthinking mind reduced to the tired "language of love."

Green becomes the morning lost equation, thoughts clouds reasoning with a heaving hidden drawl, gray as a monument mistrusting the sun. The water barely reaching the shore making its own new shore lapping up the individual stories, hypnotizing the eyes. Thoughts visual, soft words without any story traveling by fast transportation, where the eyes are fixed and the mind becomes less of a mind—a giraffe without a head.

This year soft words and more about the rich. Enough troops with more shamming brothers thinking. These people all work! Confusion as sad hands fly around the head wringing out the blood in Japanese, moving like a thick laser skimming the skin.

He's there and not, quoting the joke passage, the birth country, the inevitable return of the horse symbol and finally the necessary murder. An arrow through his walking neck. The rivers brown color packed light. Baby faces glide through the wind and then the taut face of a dog. Hot topics comes in fast detail. You boys come in from the rain.

Subbing, day packs its sun bright hot in your face. He just couldn't stop. There was no question who it was. You take it apart and it comes off easily fusing into a direct image, language in a plastic bag.

Flaked into red, duped, left with the feeling of controlled awe. As Perseus rides the head of the horse, floating the clear voyage of home.

Through the wind watching your face turning forward to meet me— the stranger. Black and orange against the season's material, as my new family gathers itself in plowing through, breaking in from the cold, while my child's mind is only with you, cold as a skeleton filled with literal good-byes. Repeating—the words floating out endlessly catching up in themselves in the dry air, in the thick dirt that holds you, while my own image gazes stupidly out against the sky hiding in the big furniture that was home.

Now the light diffuses confusing one family into the other one, into the present one that is. The eyes rely simplistically changing each posture, arms construed, faces on one anothers bodies.

Radio, fluid, the trapped jewel, trapped in saying goodbye, bringing back the cold reoccurrences, arms that stopped cold, hair standing up wild on the pillow. As if saying it, would let it settle. Only the vague sense of forgetting an expression, an arm slung around a shoulder, a stooped laugh, china, legs propped up in the languid posture of the sick. Red waves come back brighter and sunnier, picture windows of the 50's and all this in style, now camp.

So when I turn the corner I am home, this home, moving in and out for the sun thinking ocean. As if we had other names in our biased conversation; words as symbols, of how they are used. You become my location seen through gauze. Although the difference is that you are clear touchable and part of you in the present becomes my normal mother, the German studied part dissuaded, relaxed at home.

Indira lies next to you performing ritualistic details allowing herself to finally rest. These are detailed and real and in the country morning violence etches its way in glass, murder enthralled left with the light of the symbolic floor.

Different power in abstract thought, light that made noise—using the her as a substitute, an indiscriminate voice, a sort of soldier word.

There were no words of the disillusioned past. Through the words it was no coincidence in getting back. The weather showed its way. We waited to take vehicles and you don't die unless that fire. The beginning was wanting to do it and a lot of words and actions were stated. A lot of repetitious actions and words of strong feeling were severely given away. This is not fire and what isn't fire. What isn't imagined in the mind. A chicken in the bath.

Through all of Gorky's only eyes, transposing the sun through the window, overseeing the extra words, coldly executing the redundancies through his charismatic past, the past of a declining war, death marches through the aching wind.

Economy time not crossing each other. It was almost the distant past. Every day it seemed further away. Every day they talked to each other and every day it seemed to go. It went before the others like a judgement. It was always seen before them by her. It was always judged before them by her and every day it seemed to get farther and farther away. The comfort was there and it seemed to get farther and farther away. The listening was there and it seemed to get farther and farther away. It wasn't that it was moving. There was no intent. It was challenged and questioning and rationalized and angry and formulized and electric and moving away, longing to be touched. A half wrung moon.

A long low room of remembrances through which light plays. How many women love successful power eyes to mouth, back to eyes, destructive to melons. A tinge of gray. Brenda and Doris, Doris and Tommy, Tommy through Sherrie, did you hear it hit though, rotating around in nasty language. The whole truth is never known. As if everything was bathed in a cartoon light frozen in form.

The invisible woman, no longer accurate stands, milk lapping up her legs, thinks words cut.

What kind of poem?

A mechanical doll, term used before describing some man, now aimed directly at the two men trying to kill each other after indirectly killing her. In a different language, some foreign one as if some made it more decisive, desirous, a practicality.

Write the alphabet in theory so each letter in substance is vague, not glazed out from too much sentiment but sentiment holding it together.

Effortless and thoughtless the Ophelia symbol makes the application, takes derangement showing it publicly, pulling it out and then raking it back in; thick movements, machine like with her hands and legs pulling herself around in a circle fish knives forming a halo around her head. Delicate through faulty error. A bag over her head. In the dark columned room, decisions are made.

Slaughtering liabilities, a commodity practiced equation. As a second language, as if can't reach, could not extend, would not be left an empty pulsing thing.

Technology as slice broadening towards the computer image of Polonius lurking in the background, the maternal fetal lot as blue as it plays.

Radiating in finger guns and the tiny paragon of family life, not believing the ones whose horses appear slowly, by themselves, but letting them come. We could all exaggerate our tongues making them cows' tongues, brows intact, until the agitated shore redirects itself, allowing paradise to reappear.

The Letters

July 23, 1976

Dear Peter,

To sever unknown qualities
There is little to say unless taken lightly.
He walked in wearing a heavy gold cross, and asked to stay in the
room.
That music was not for him to hear.
I walk out humming a Puerto Rican number.
The boys all know that one.
It is a failure being a different tune.
He still asks to stay.
Maybe the elevator will break.
Maybe we will all forget our pasts and ethnic backgrounds.
Maybe the only true Americans are Protestants.
Line fractions small cuts, here is luck in the purest sense.
A bright streak of light flashes from his cigarette turning us
formally ecstatic until another one is smoked.
You see, he quotes, "Far enough into the forest there is always
more to see."
In Europe all the lights are out. Everyone has two birthdays.
Thinking his would never occur he goes to visit his wife as much
as possible, soon they will marry again.
I resign myself to passing images; turn on and off in a second.

I no longer feel guilty but wonder how long I will allow myself to be robbed.
The only successful implement is the first thought although the rest explains.
I need to leave when that one comes on.
No more party games.
Once Is Not Enough
All of the young women become innocent in thought and want only to be spared.
The men become teachers and each sex is satisfied and disgusted.
They have become so conservative.

Lynne

August 13, 1977

Dear Hank,

With a different crowd do jocks get in the way? His voice as it used to be. A strong chain for good luck, vowels into attention, youngsters in their single twenties. Ocean City is for lovers. I'm one chance away, great strangers at night. Diversity of his kingdom, hear monolithic language harmonizing sounds.

He takes the recorder then slips away. I felt he didn't care yet the holiday had just begun. He sat across from me while his own hand held his beautiful arm. It became increasingly clear now who I was with. He did almost everything with care but unknowingly. He had no sisters. He had a business of his own. Being completely opposite I felt concern, near laughter, near expense, near television, an acute entertainment of his body. I wondered about boredom. I wondered about basketball, and if height thrown at the exact moment could execute a mere two points, my own ability to be near and closed.

His hair slicked back became almost fashionable slightly off course. I felt he need not be so reserved. In uniform between commercials he was quite convincing. He would lie down and be interesting. Being protected by a lady was worth the trip. Yet I wanted him, one more accusing factor. It gets stale and takes time, it needs a quiet view

Touch dry land   expressive tombstones

gift clarity

anchorage dream blood residue

    lot crevices

September-memory month

We picked him out right away. The June Taylor Dancers. Donny and Marie's Roller Skating Review.

I'm just visiting-mambo 3 step.

And she lives her- pseudo retail store.

Billy Kilmer- party and it doesn't matter how, bus trolley journey. Make checks restore all locked doors. Cute and fancy the girl next door, reserved I can still see, a new kind of tune replaces the new. The text is able to protect. Skipping off into married life telephone signals become extinct.

Leesberg.

Kathleen Blake: accounting: Board Room.

4a. Characterized by a dazed irresponsive state, impulsively or obsessively quick to use something.

in and out- the long nose resting on his paws: Virginia Woolf trigger happy

In my mirror in the morning I must do nothing to arouse them. Korda insisted but no one must see. He had no right turning his back on Levin, the custodian of the rights of men.

He was quiet. In my own words it included my

winter-entrance album.

more uniform disease. .

He looked at me skeptically and said, "Yes, you do a little too much of that. You don't talk too much. You've got to win to get the seat back. You're interesting. You're short. You've got long straight hair. You can call. You can say without pleasure. You can hide. Are you leaving? Are you a T.V. addict? Are you entertained? Are you sleeping? Are you supreme? Are you a fancy dream? Are you the hypnotists fame and future? Are you into it?"

Lynne

September 27, 1976

Dear Tina,

But add a touch of pain in Rome.
I am with you.
Yell devotion!
Do the Freddy in 76.
He was impressed with that.
He fell in love with you for that.
And then you opened
Your eyes-where they are.
Now I'm moved by separate poems.
Electric music will also come to understand your most extreme
desires.
You yourself said it's such an inside thing.
I'm not so sure.

Love always,
Lynne

October 6, 1976

Dear Kenny,

I was quiet, secure, lucid, and happy.
I was taking a trip.
I was stating things interestingly.
I was interesting.
I was small.
Some of them don't speak.
I didn't want to do everything.
Bernice's cousin read the note and exploded. I was thankful for his care.
She confiscated the thermos.
She always threatened.
She became serenely emotional.
She released and objected.
She was militant.
She continued the salute.
To sketch you abstract I'd like your face to show it.
In my apartment.
In my logbook, they become almost alive. I surrendered, pertaining to attire-the usable past.
Pertaining to luck, new styles in holsters.
Pertaining to accent, corruption of literary supplements.
Pertain-reflex.

First I carried jars filled with every possible motive of action. Next came the freedom to use it. I examine it. I stretch it. I digest. I try. I disguise.

Then you foreshadowed small events and it was lovely. Then you turned your subsequent wrist. I keep busy and I'm boring. I walk too. I answer everything in money. Not finding understanding it becomes a masquerade. The reason, lyrical turn of sympathy. Anything goes in a musical review. Pakistan is too far in the stars. A happy juror becomes one. He packs the helmet and then puts it on his head bent in prayer. I become more interested in what I'm saying. I believe, catch, and apply. It's alright to the square root, continuation of the 9th degree. Recapturing the mood, he turns the lighting down. Autobiography read easily. It has begun, next week is nice.

Lynne

October 8, 1977

Dear Andrew,

Don't worry, the machines are working well, all of the tension has dissipated. I keep thinking what would happen if I did move. I mean me with all of my emotionalism and you and your Chinese hangings from Zayre's. It's not that I'm knocking them, I mean I understand the need but how do you capture over-abundance versus acute withdrawal.

It's you and it's not you. I like it and hate it but I feel you're trying the impossible, please just be sincere.

I've begun some of the projects again, in fact some of the moodiness has disappeared. Can you see it has nothing to do with, "I'm sure you've never had trouble meeting the opposite sex." It seems something more internal with you. As for your children, Colorado isn't really that far.. Mr. Early said himself, "You might be just what we need" I hope so, could really use the change down South. People are well you know friendlier.

I can't seem to accentuate what I'm saying. If you are that tense you would touch me lightly. If you were that tense you couldn't move or you wouldn't stop moving. You feel right. I don't want you to look away. I want you to lay down. I want you to be bored and still want me around. I want to be unpleasant and real. I mean I can think of you in Trenton but you're too nice and I can't accept it. Stop me in turquoise. Lift it up. Praise lovely blondes. I see your quietness. I want you to lay down. I see sugar on a tiny spoon. I learn how to inhale.

If he's only interested in language, why does he admire my work.. I swear I can understand the strength of what he's saying but not what he's saying. He always looks at the point below my eyes and then glances up.

He makes me self conscious. I always need to look back. There is something obvious, ridicule to free his thoughts, no need for induced laughter. Then everyone moved to California. It was delicious. I felt lovely, almost special. I didn't have a care in the world. I stepped into the ocean, the fire lit up, creating sporadic leaps and pictures.

The old musician put down his fiddle, and come towards me, softly placing his rose in the sand. My past disappeared. I felt concern, I wanted everything satisfied. I wanted to receive pleasure infinitely I walked towards him watching for jagged edges of rock and undertow. The lizards were not haunting but encircled my legs casting a certain trance over my body. Feeling their motion I was no longer afraid. Darling, don't worry, I've come home and I'm not afraid. If I meet them in town I will merely nod a pleasant day.

Lynne

October 19, 1976

Dear Ron,

Then you foreshadowed small events and it was lovely.
Then you became the accusing factor and resisted.
Then you listed all phrases containing I and closed the door.
You kept eye-mind concentration from disintegrating.
Then you answered completely and became a friend.
Then you surrounded yourself with books and picked carefully through.

I began to think of you as the objective matrix- you became visible
tough in my eyes.
I resisted strategy while the cathedral shifted its personality.
I ate a big meal and calmed down.
I wrote a story and lifted my bed.
I didn't T.V.

Take the volley playfully away.
The intention becomes very clear. I could easily hold them in my
hand.
I didn't need to laugh. I spoke less.
I extracted the moment and defined it flatly.
You began the laborious task. I sat astonished, and openly refused.
You were friendly as a teacher.
You examined the work and were patient, more or less disregard.
I find him in his own business.
I find him characteristically still.
I find him less removed than I thought.
I study language more seriously. For the first time I hear a word
spoken.
I can tell by the uplift of his voice.
His body quivers, he asks for direction. He counteracts the decision.
He counteracts the decision and asks why. Next all of the restaurants
close. I want to move a pretty picture—human relationships.
I want to phase out performance—Mack the Knife,
Celia—woman, direction of crafts.
Maurice and performs olympically. I can do all of them.

Strategically, I fall from a more secure place. There is a method in my task.

How to occupy the allotted space with more precise language.

With more precise language it is no longer necessary to find out who committed the crime. I become patient, more exact in each action. Whereas before I was controlled by this I am now the controlling factor. I feel safe, powerful. I stop joking around. I look at everyone so now they turn away embarrassed. I'm not afraid. I'm in control.

I want the message less contorted, the action replaces any word.
Next I want to silence the world but yet you talk.
You examine the worthiness.
You alone have charisma.
You alone make sense.
You become the story, crime, talisman, and each symbol on the board.
You are the quoted interest in each comment.
I immediately exit and become recreationally relaxed. I am only satisfied in the sauna.

Next I capture movement depicting the ratio of atomic elements, time, place, weather conditions, nonreferential sets separate. You're skeptical and quick.
I release inertia, Blake softly.

Lynne

October 25, 1977

Dianne,

I think I know you, don't pass slowly when you become secretly lost and satisfied.
When I find you silly and drunk, your voice distinct.
Invite opposite eyes, immediate gratification.
A combination, skillful ice.
Then nothing in my favor, and I become the I in each of my stories.
And somehow your Kansas dreams are equally real. Would you tear your delightful glance backwards, or sideways like your mouth performs?
It's hard to listen while my eyes perform less difficult tasks.
I forget how to think.

I'm not that ancient gorilla in the park. I become the traveler, meet beautiful strangers once a night.
I follow light one more quiet mood. I'm out of my niche. I like it.
I follow light, one more quiet mood. I like it.

Lynne

November 29, 1976

Dear Craig,

I'm not the junkie that moves to England. I become wholesome self destruct in a second. I keep thinking of red hair and I don't know why. I've known you behind bars, on the roof and now the circular tower becomes almost real. All I need is a cigarette.

Please, don't treat me with so much compassion, I may begin to believe you and these days I've trained myself to just sit dazed on the floor with my feet propped up on the wall. I'm not home and I am. I remember my eyes but when I look into them they become empty, and then I want blue ones so I too can be distant and serene.

The Unitarian's dilemma becomes clear. New York is a desperate city. She laughs so much that I can't even talk to her anymore. The peacocks fly in from India, I etch quietly. The move to England is canceled. I examine profusely, sluggish at my own risk, an attempt at friendship. At the corner a kiss away.

In the columbian junkyards I find them playing, the two divorcees completing their act. Bocaccio's repulsed, Sara moves underground. I take long strides.

The rest of the crowd have revealed their tragedies, on the wall my own list becomes inclusive. I'm still astonished at the possibilities of my life. It's you and it's not you. The animals run wild. The next second I fall in love. I can tell by the line in his eye he too sometimes forgets.

I choose people against car parts, the latter bearing that pleasant liquid warmth. Don't take my arm and spotlight away. I like the weight. I become the drugged culture, sublime. I become the aggressor lost in the city street. I negate, go to the country and listen to the back door slam no longer needing to be that free. I play with death it's only a joke to the survivors. I become my own closet.

Your eye-contact becomes you but it's the real things I'm questioning, the house not a quaker hurt, not a set-back game, not carry-over value, not a score card, not aggression, regression, or a chord in a depressed state, not a depressed state, not trigger happy, not happy, not illusive, and not extinct, not within character, not humble, no withdrawal, not personality, no direction, not limitless, not demolition, and not without a crowd carousing on New Year's Eve, not a snowy tree, a picture of a pretty girl walking down the road smiling, not filling that up, not being inquisitive and not watching and not listening no and you feel good too. We speak at the same time, I can't hear and I like it. My memory in El Paso is clear. Junk compared to a penguin mothering her young. . It becomes a quiet reflection. I'm in touch, clean.

You become that plurality of escapes, an open room and patterns become boring. Next to the office I dress, another effortless reaction. Stoically release, love, humor me. One baby unit. The moment he needs the book you comfort, turn, speak, and stop mortifying yourself. I no longer pull strings from the top of my head, the last time for calm dexterity. Break softly into larger products, let integrity diminish. All of us become extremely arid and meet uptown, serious and armed.

I sit waiting, given sound, the exact replica of your face. If he's jovial he may be right. I leave ceremonial pavements of my mind. I have a place to live and it looks like you, the words don't come as easy. I'm not the baby in the hospital and I'm embarrassed. You're far. I've read and noticed but I don't believe it.. Only love at first sight with its shirt sleeves rolled up, serious, challenged, and neat.

You're adorable decked out in your chains. Wrap the moonlight. Create small laughter. A delicate balance. For Rose Marie I create new off-spring and most of them are applying names, lasting character images. I no longer follow the distance of poetic words. I speak for a moment and flare silently, ignoring photosynthetic atmosphere.

Lynne

December 18, 1976

Dear Celia,

It's all becoming clear. The spotlight you sent, the exact lettering of the card, and now even your expression. It's funny like when my own words run wild and everyone laughs. I see detail and in your head- art completes, repetitive like a funny incident.

I'm out now. The silence is wonderful, sometimes hearing that tiny voice. Books crack down on the right side of my shoulder, and I'm relaxed.

No Ceil, I don't want to tell you my past or mixed relations, it's not important with you. I hear the scorched replacement and that's enough. Sometimes at the hospital I hear it when everyone's gone and it's just the boarders and me. I get happy and need to let them out of their cages.

I'm almost free. It's words and it's not. That clean excitement, the two disks against pink, and then I feel uplifted and light. I think sometimes I'm falling down only to catch the gay little emotionalism on the third step. Then his voice catches me and I can once again start the climb. I wanted to tell you, actually needed to tell you how I've needed our closeness, but now everyone's only interested in how well they're doing. No more excitement in the streets. I've been to Texas and back and still yearn for that last galloping detail.

As for love, I've thought about at times but then the "Third World" interrupts. I become revolutionary and crave excitement.

That one slip of the forehead and it's over. Equalities become prevalent, and I can't enjoy, only react with oxygen and words to hear myself become alive. That small slice of compassion, even the smile comes through, the
corner soft commercial
raspy jewel thief
the blank ad-man
acidseized musician and Buzz Aldrin
I identify with all of them and can understand austerity, winter, and Divine, you too, in your divine and velvet pants.

I'm sometimes all arms and ready to slip out for a couple of minutes a day. I've so many things to start, I've got to start running. Write soon, I miss you.

Love,
Lynne

December 18, 1976

Dear Danny,

I'm not sure about the paper, samba towards the nth degree. All of the pineapples are frozen, the South American beauties moving only from the waist up, their faces strong and beautiful, high cheek bones suggest. It's practically you, making me feel again, not just slouched out in the tender West. You leave it up to me.

Down south amble through. I'm in a setting quarantined, the bed takes up the whole room. I don't have to push, you can look at me or the mirror, aim the knife and fix, beauty.

I'm not fragile, but walk on the edge, dance, extreme positions. Next I grow three more feet, and explain reason externally. One day on the roof I'm not embarrassed, I ride the elevator all night, cats, crawling on the floor, the red blanket on the chair, the knife aimed at the wall, 1500 dollars for pagoda glass.

So is it really the fine things in life that matter. Some day you're a rich man, a chance of a life time. Doreen's taking long rides in her new Porsche and it hasn't broken down yet. The discipline catches up in her little finger. She's trying not to make scenes. It's hard being that emotional and calm at the same time.

The new art gallery is beautiful, everything is sleek and slim. Evacuation of the 30's, little patterns on the wall. During the war the woman will cut their hair, all of the dogs go underground. We're put out of business, the long straight line.

Sometimes I'm the rubberband man. I just don't care, vacillate between that tarnished smell and a wide open day. You catch yourself then turn still away, socially. I want to dance with you, then you ruin my excitement while shifting your weight. I become serious and react. Expression minimizes with my silly attitude.

Drink soup, flash symbolically. My mouth becomes full, fingers exact, magazine style. I'm too emotional and I know it. Try a Little Tenderness, my kind of poetry. Shift gears in columbia and pain. Feline distemper, foams at the mouth, an opening age. The rest of the description is negated. I float into the beautiful bathroom while your Polish maid glances sideways. I hear her typing, flatten my reaction, become a stairwell in the distant apartment, garage below.

Yes, I too become delicate and strong. I take such care. Combine actuality to reason, did you make the weasel on the stone? Write when you get there.

Lynne

P.S. Tuffy's little breakdown coincided with all of the other problems around the house. There wasn't room for anyone, my own excitement increased preoccupied with each individual's drama. It seemed to matter what they were saying but the magazines edited all of it, they didn't think it made interesting literature.

I felt different. The readings were like a croquet game, competition subtle. I'm in a quiet mood and nicer to the dogs. Why is the relationship of a human to his animal funny, almost like a small childs and I never thought of that as funny. He looked at me in his little Santa costume and both of us knew who was the crazy one.

The sugar craze, obviously I agree, am reacting obviously. The nun's waiver, you limit the confusion, compassion resumes underground. Next all of the babies explode, are calm, and happy. Yes I'm more myself, sugar in the morning, the crunch bunch, shake and bake. The bouncing, needle from chair to arm. Blood brothers. Mesmerized I walk back over Wisconsin towards the University. All of the strong men vanish. I'm in a field the breeze blowing, languid, still, releasing short orders.

A sultry past. All of it comes down when you leave and your voice gets excited, eyes cast down.

Dilantin- knowledge of direction
Mylepsin- wonder lust
Dilantin- becomes extremely careful
aminopholine- a nice day
ascorbic acid- testing
Butozolidin- game retriever
Cambiotic- cannibal life
picture = picture
word = sentence
mood = manner
sanitation flush = California nomad land
California nomad land = a Coke float.

February 13, 1977

Dear Korda,

Always in my eyes the vertical baby becomes the king. He gives himself then runs past the machines. Seven birds scatter nervously on the snow, on their way to someone else. You're mod and the laces are tied securely. Suburban trees grow upward. A moment of ecstacy and Missy plunges to her death. The school board reneges. I want to crush you, then leave you alone. A light prism stadium, reflection in the outlined field.

Everyone's in search of the industrial sensitive city, greetings at the corner store.

Delirium 3 and I'm in it.

A hat says he's one.

Then your eyes stare numbly ahead, you speak, another word for country music, as I sit back sober and pale.

Love may bring a toast of wine, farewell my lovely and more than human. There is a similar lowering of voices, decorated, it's not apathy and it's not local, the parade lasting far into the night.

I must reacquaint myself, the clearness of taking attention, swirling lightly over the eggs, painting and more jealous action. Anything that I have missed, guidance, practicality, and trust. The cats return all over the floor, readjusting their weight. The robins hide when the people come. Filled with good intentions morning takes my answers, I speak discussing medicines, the possibility of a lingering New Year. I become a pony down in all fours.

More time and more understanding-spectate.

I'm imagining the operation, a smile that begins deep in my throat then curdles its way right into my eyes forgetting the mouth relapsing into an upturned grin.

Mechanical chickens could not attract the lonely. Sharks react, his piece about movies, an aquatic reaction to the money involved. Next came the choice of literature. It was more common than the retroactive beauty of an attractive girl. It had something to do with deep down where the feelings begin.

Write what, eight late. She took my arm and guided me fast into the bar mumbling something about her leaving for Uganda the next day. The midgets gyrated on the table tops flirting with the bigger people. All of us had made it, this was the charmed dream come true, the great billowy dream come true. The beginning of a New

Year. A time to start. I howl a more anxious tune to the wind. On the porch I can almost see you caring for the dogs, bringing them the paper for their cages. Muscle against muscle, a pinned leg.
Anaesthesia wears off and Bayles interrupts.
A genius.
Wait patient   Stored knowledge
14th and U   You almost become a gentleman, one I can accept, trying to classify the liquid into eight specific crystal slices.
Primitive-prime time
Leisurely   You're my fancy dancer. Disco tech   Retrospect.

In the cage the eyes only visible. Named characters meant more. A suggestion something new for the dogs, millions of cases of lonely friendly silly portable people. Next time I see you I come to collect. Next time is nice.

Lynne

February 29, 1977

Carmen,

Stop!

Don't stop!

Stress volumes are at full velocity. Now I'm embarrassed and logical, everything seems to come down to two choices, fact or fantasy the arrangement of time and the management of money.

I'm working at it, the weather has finally broken the past couple of days, complicating all of us with age. And in your eyes the tragic sense of surprise.

I used to see it sometimes when the cats were ready to leave, you bringing them out, such concern I had not thought possible.

Cupid stays locked up in the gas station, another one of my flaky attitudes. I trust again sacrificing my own knowledge at the expense and regard of aesthetic beauty, coolness, and style. Security or comfort, my first memory the sun on my skin feeling warm and not caring.

Anxious persuasion- a chronicle.

Shadow boxing- a comedy. I search beside and inside of me, trying to make a name without meaning anything. It becomes a selfish game. Lone drinks blood, another way to deal with loneliness.

Oscillating tendencies, a crazy horse.

I'm beginning to understand a little of memory, how we can remember things in one sense, then the memory becomes present and it's not memory at all, the present act becomes the memory of the incident and the memory becomes the action the memory becomes. It has nothing to do with daydreaming but more to do with writing and writing, with what I'm trying to do with writing, and talking.

It fits.

Well, they do all the cute things or they know each other so well they don't really have to speak or they use each other so well they're both extremely happy or she takes care of him or he takes care of her and they both care and they both conclude it.

Or he picks her up in the Marriott, and listens to the Muzak and listens to the MUzak ooooooooooooo kkkkkkkkkkkkkkkk and they give each other knowing glances and everything is secure and right.

And everything is secure and right, and skip the summer and go into the government and the government becomes logical and emotional and I want to listen and I need to talk and I have to get his opinion and dress up and dress down and make an impression and the Shakespeare Festival is alone and frozen and great.

All metabolic processes stop. First the heart, pulse, and cyanosis becomes one. The New American Marriage. He works. She works. Father out mother dead sisteroutbrotherand the sardonic sergeant and the T.V. are one together.

Again I'm back with the mongoloid-Time.

Lean Expectation

Soothing the skin that came in   slower and thicker
the fish that changed slowly to be a man and Martino too slowly at
the wall, a rag a favorite portrait of himself.

Lynne

Tamoka

Part 1

The little spotted dog licks the adoptees forms.
The fat girl reads the Avon booklet.
The skinny waitress drags a Parliament.

Melancholia — closed visual perspective (pronoun)

Lynne Dreyer — insincere noise (listen)
Cleverly living our interesting lives (dumbstruck)

An old lady in synopsis in a pink bouffant pink hat.

Certain people whom I have known strike a similar pose. I usually can accept by allowing them to read my mind, inserting their own use of free words and poetry, such as a prescribed method, language or device, as in red inducing passion or black and lonely — a picture postcard one that I can really see. I want my poetry understood, as if someone was interested in getting to know me. Then we can be silly and close.

Not one of our favorites, delicately placed.

Baggage identification. I remember the day I started the trip, standing in Alexandria. Your jeans are somewhere floating around in Texas. Can't write anymore, but think it's o.k., a duel book, upside down, perfect friends. I'm glad you're going now, no more wondering about what could have been, if I had been less judgemental, less like myself. No more watching and denying my own feelings. How you found me in my own corner, deep in the center of my brain, the way you bring lightheartedness to situations, an overall view, practicality.

You've changed now and I'm glad although jealous that I couldn't be a part of it. It had something to do with failure or the ability for you to really try; you said it was upbringing or religion. I disagreed and laughed and cried while watching the sun in Brooklyn.

Money, self-destruction, metabolism, large major things, we always included these in our discussions, the real stuff was felt, your ability to change style, give almost selflessly, explain your life in terms of detail. But when you started to laugh I was out, a different ball game. I couldn't be honest and didn't think you cared if I was or not.

Self-contained, artists, family life, and all along me moving different images in my mind, wanting to give you something.

Stooped work.

Don't be shy now. We can read along together on this one. From chicks to women to ladies, the Arbella. "I always think it's more honest and provocative to be genuinely autobiographical, but maybe that's just me." Is Lanier Place named after Sydney Lanier?
Wish your father was here.
Pictures-a masterpiece.
Hope you're well and happy.
Hope you're getting on well with the cats and plants.
Hope you're doing well.
Hope to see you at the Big Reading.
Hope you're having luck in your job search.
Hope this finds you well.
Hope all is well with you. Hope you're able to find a better job.

Rob a typewriter.

The chimpanzee throws you a kiss from the condominium in

Florida. Years of business from Baltimore to Chicago to Baltimore, selling all the sports equipment and in your outgoing and comical way, the family saddened by the death, not coming to the funeral, only wanting the minks and clothes and perfume, a glamorous pose. Implement the torn black and silken cloth, implement the torn, washing your hands and small chairs and then always again making it light. When you think how great it is to be alive.

But as soon as I say it both of you come back into my mind. Any other relationship seems only partial and fanciful like decorated with what clothes I should wear, the atmosphere, who else is present, looks, detailed comparisons of the sixties to the seventies, tv, talk of the future, a family.

I try to ignore it, not think about it, become like you, not expect things, don't smoke, become someone else, become helpless, become helpful, be comical, grin, extract memory, get skinny, get fat, be healthy, be only a voice, a vacuole, a moving microplasm on the bus, play a little game of teacher cashier writer and none of these ever becoming games, but like a picture postcard which suggests a certain memory, blue gayne, and illicits memory suggestive to a specific place, "Greetings from the Cozy Motel," Thurmont, Maryland.

I remember you in certain intense situations. The only thing is the players are all wrong. The feeling becomes as contrived as the piece of paper it's written on and placed. I become quiet.

Isn't life grand? Sounds like Irish, sounds like Oh, protection, sounds like someone else will pick me up and I'll go, sounds like this time I'm really not wanting to be alone like in the dream traveling from Baltimore, or dead Presidents captioned on the postcard, the East Potomac Park, describing language.

What I see in him is a seriousness and that seems most important now not funny jokes or making me feel comfortable, topsy turvy, switch, empty apartments, jungle life.

Oh, don't argue with me now. I just need you to look out of the window with me. It's difficult to write about you both separately.

How the timing was wrong, how I never really saw your attempt at making things pleasant for yourself, our beneficial likeness, sight. But none of it matters more than the fact of me denying that I felt anything more than friendship with you. Your one attempt at boldness, telling me I was wrong. Playground days, a doer. Under the tree sexual talks, a suggestion, dead Presidents, replica of arguments, messenger life and resolved pleasantries after convincing you to come back with me. And that is what I despised the most. Picture postcards from the coffee shop. Letters from Yates, wingshaped legs, a cynical cowboy, better than all of that long hair.

Oh, don't argue with me now, how what I really loved was the way you would argue with me, in a way I could accept, so that a certain amount of freedom recalled. Our too critical look at each other. A gain music, a purple people eater, a strong cylinder, a man of your word.

Flash image, people made of cement yakking wildly on the bus image, the ladies in white drinking tea from miniature tea-cups their hair flying off from the tops of their heads, image, the wild cat waiting for me to get some air, image, his pleasant voice only pursued in the machines, the pigs and dogs all herded together in the den. South Euclid, Honey, Ohio, trips, no more black thoughts, Ode to Billy Joe, bugs a sergeant, image the fish leading the girls by the pool, Haiti, oranged and snow in California, a job of madrigals. Be Bop A Loop Bop, tomorrow at the Boy's Ranch it's where you're going that counts, the black hand tougher in structure but more vulnerable in terms of what it's saying. You're right, I really do have to be in touch with what I'm feeling for the writing to come off.

A testimonial dessert, an acrobatic walk, a physical sunset, an introverted embrace, an accomplished necklace, a stained reaction, an honest V neck, a fractional chance, patient books, directional success, an individual doll, an open carnival, sympathy, crystal methodology, humorous dogs.

Part 2

The locker room aid dances to the radio distraction.
Lost visibility one walking rain.
Sliced vanity serious charm ice.
An economic situation a story.

When she smiles another star is lit saline, floral, ragine shark.
Necessary understanding of sensory input.

When she laughs, she drops the cheese; Little Big Bear Caw Caw Caw,
hasting modification of sensory interpretations.

Carrying swollen branches that drip in the wind responsive states,
a unique way of working today.

going on stage with a needle in her head biography
reject equivalent of response
overtime the leaves

The digital reflex of the brain becomes classic, wasted directed to
the retina to aggravate the ending.

Exaggerate the ending.

Large non-concrete words form a deep cylindrical well.
Who likes a poetic voice? The Phantom gets tired of Takoma,
socialism and work.

A loose myth, a structured fairytale, an equivalent voice.
"A love spills it."
Helpless as in continued conversation, his mother's voice.
The point of the body of a drowning victim at the point where the
brain stops receiving blood.

"A love spills it."
A raccoon on all fours hanging from a tree, hands in prayer, a secretary bird, hands clapping a date palm, a blue and yellow macaw, a chinese gong, the right hand buttoning a glove on the left hand, the left hand buttoning the glove on the right hand, a stone tower lighthouse, a hopscotch, a creel, a beehive hairdo, a modern windmill, the left hand peeling skin from the right hand, the right hand peeling skin from the left hand.

Part 3

On Sunday I have Thursday I'm dressed right. On Sunday it's Thursday. Potion Love. Murder skin parts of the body of course. Segments fall, this one time, this one time, where solitude mixes with slower reaction, with slower thought and memory, and memory fades for country, silence lingers, trips to the cabinet, vials emptied, to kill, to silence and start. Start one more, one more I'm done. I'm away, one more I'm away.

The family pitifully waives food for television. All fades, all memory. At once I'm done, this time think of her small ways, her small acts. The rest of the machine stops, sounds like rain. In small cities, it's slower, it takes longer to go. Go for, go for. At the entrance all moved, each remembers. I'm still her, I'm still here. Containers of loved ones fall securely away. This is strange and near. I rush candy to play, to bring harmony to remember you, to remember you to play not so hard, to remind you to stop playing. In the middle of the left hand corner I thank her. I'm again.

I can laugh at important things.

Fallen ash to air as in words and worlds. Name drop I can I can. All of them have short hair, the homes turn placidly away. They keep clean, keep change in small time and metabolism becomes faster and stronger with vanity. He says all women are sometimes vain and size changes to metabolism to keep them going, to keep them clean. Words form a videotape winter. A new type of nervousness sets in, a grunt here and there.

Cold and arranging are meant to be perfectly still. Sometimes it's hard for me to see you. Storage light goes on. I'm out. I'm away. Storage light goes away. Experiment that to pictures, to their deep Books of the Indian now Spanish, now half breeds, now p.h.

Never will see you whole, never will see you moving. Her skin changed white and then she turned around, being always that way in public. She never answered that, foursome to believe. A ham.

Not to be meaningful right. I'm back to where I am. Forget dreams. The sound of music and some easy words are left very still. A new car and a cheap hotel and MTM enterprises, new and old American women still calling her boss Mr. with paper and still, and still coming on. An issue.

Hold a dollar bill yet perfectly still. In a few months life will change drastically for some people and still come back to cities. Ideas reply sigh brother trust refuses deals I proved I'm wrong, everyone can remember their bodies equal to hold, hold water, laughter sin, and off-stage bows. Where we were, the gangster regime. I accept. The sun goes down in a smaller state.

Journalize the ant. Love is so amazing, creep into my dreams. Pearls rewards, could be alike could be serious, serious to play, jealous and simple. My head is cramped with days. I can see the storage space, I can see spring and you've got a friend. I know the buildings will be here longer, that they forget mistakes and understand that you never return to the living with so much to offer with so much reward with much to hold back with no more secrets and nothing to lose.

"Southern Journey" and the small frame of books. The cancer of small cells, their unnatural disaster and their want to conquer, to shave heads and bring certain chemicals to equilibrium, extent of pity.

When I want him. Separate parts back to these small sounds.

My eyes where they become one with my past, more to tell before realistic subjects. The point of wonder, wonder lust, Wonder talk, magic of certain toys. Pictures wait nocturnally. I sit astonished. The bee love child. Solid. Shammin'. Swak.

Play it somewhere else. Don't be shy now.

Says discreetly, says failures, says the sun without its name being part of it. Seems today brings lots of surprises without my body becoming part of it. What I've always thought necessary and tried.

If it's slower, I'm cheating and don't find out and want to come back. If it's slower, I'm cheating and don't find out for one week. Everything happens in one day. I become classified and return to the city. Everything was more prominent, no one took walks at night. Sugar milk, milk sugar. He wants protection.

Reprise out in the country; she becomes her daughter. Well admits love when safe away.

Coming completely, deduct lovely thoughts, style shows it, hemlines where they used to be, romance is back, families are here to stay, they come to counteract and biography will never bore me. Execute tv.

Prompt delivery, anxious still, write forward, flatter, I love to imitate violent men. It always seems to work. They play walrus on the path, stops my breathing, I'm in two places. I'm in a doctor's office waiting to be taken, I'm also in a box, this time caged in, this time lasting, this time whole, I try to think of another way to be.

Major Helpurn. Master Charge. Major change.

The Sabrina hotel, and you looking like royalty without the crown on your head.

Lingo street, cool lingo, street under. Obviously fancy, now talk out loud talk out athletics.

Locker room disease. Our black man on top of the world, sounds complete, sounds pronoun. He said things real, he said histories, he said his son, cat's chin, blond and strawberry hair, strawberries and cream. Prompt rescue, better slight without. This is sure and close, this next one moves, this one is stronger yet closed.

Sure and move into other kingdoms, frantic motions are causing some meticulous split of the personality in two. At two it continues. Hand moving short hands, my hands bleed. With drink the entire scene changes. He seems to watch and care.

Looks like Hendrix and is completely still.
He was study. He stayed late. Leave out musically. Leave out mandolins. Leave out pleasant memory.

Firebirds sign out formally. I watch and exaggerate biography to the fullest degree.

Picked African bodies down. Arms raised what camps in over twenty years, what lasting memories, what families have silenced and ran. Fabrics and laughter. He spoke of damage, initiation into the object. The comics decree of the now world, the green hornet. In the society of gravel I fall. Reaction equals mediocrity, her marriage, her undying love. Her sense of before and after affects me before anything really occurs, prevention, nutrition. It's excellent, it's never been done, no soft swinging vowels, no symbols, just the honest laceration of a lovely space.

Part 4

The electric night becomes the morning. Silly birds sing.
Drink.
The immaculate lover loves, my first American friend.
No spiders react to the solemn span of my attention.
A unique presentation and how oblique and sorry we are that
  you must go through this pain.

Ninety percent of the people become friends. The impossible
  begins to occur.
Repeat. Take the tape and camera and go to the supermarket.
Make the invisible talisman work for you. And smile and don't be

funny and smile as if you don't mean anything. You'll do alright stay up.

That clean smile, oh no the compassionate smile, not the condescending one, no the encouraging smile, the understanding smile, the sly and calculating one, the one where you've thought about it, the encompassing one that makes me scared to talk, the one when you tease me, the one where we both don't understand and we know it's o.k. and you look to me like a silent bird latched up onto a purple sky.

Part 5

You correct the change and become lost, soloing down 495 on foot, taking elaborate snapshots of the expressway signs.
Freak, friend, lover, Takoma, Takoma!
Friend who suddenly catches my disguise and brushes off my needing it, out of concern.
An easy jewel. Hey life, you got it.
A mother and one lover with two friends and a brother, someone to look up to and laugh becomes knowing well.

And this one is silly and the water will cleanse you. Warm. Long arms and legs. A new type of nervousness sets in. A grunt here and there.

Part 6

When I press my open fingers towards you.
When you eat the payroll in contempt.
When I exact the meaning of your voice.
When you become serious.
When you suggest.
I wanted you to understand.
No more time, dear, and become anonymous and becomes an
    imitation, and becomes suggestive to style.
The white tiger gets his medicine in darts, macrodantin, no
    time for poor baby.
The tall black lifeguard goes to the ocean and into it, walks and
    enjoys his life with a lady of average size.
He winks cool with understanding. Tomorrow I'll bring you a
    dime and you can pick up the trash under the tree.
Where's the White House? Oom a Loom Boom Ba Boom. Hard
    to say it, you first.

Desireless, shammin', swak.

Part 7

The room was ok in the nightime.
The muscular guy tries to fly.
The conference room is neglected.
The receptionist fills the prescription for the rabbit.
The baby gurgles, crocking up his head as if to notice. The
parents separate and kiss.
    The parents separate and kiss. Dinner is completed.
The dinner is memorable. Upsetting the tone, he gobbled up his

beets and hesitated to speak. Some foods when you really enjoy them. He stopped the music then asked a lot of personal questions. Mostly day sheets, I thought the circular brush was necessary.

Part 8 "Of a Tendency Closed Off"

A cubicle of an urban voice teasing sarcastically, whittling her nose. (sanctioned flax)

The hand is trapped. In Maine relaxed skinny, funny lovely, outgoing, earnest, a surgical papier-mache. (doctoral madness)

Not as empty animals. When they won't talk about it, do they really know about it, staking it, riding it, writing it, writing into the language, getting into it, feeling it. Does it become objective, stationary, an argument placed, a nervous set of laughs? When I check baby eyes, whose arms, snow.

They are traveling, standing on the bridge looking up. There is the water where the gulls attack. Bonita Light, being there difficult to dress at the moment, a rag hanging over the bulb that suggests concern for the voices that collaborate around it. A need, rainholes, manholes, a highly autobiographical and long piece.

Something new you. The cat licks his feet and then licks his feet again.

Sex with a Western twang.

84 4

84 4

84 4

Swing, the lifestyle depends on how you want it, beautiful. I contract, it squints, when it tries to speak seriously to hide things, becomes white, funny presents are received, no more smells and a memory, a catechism and guilt, both welfare, headquarters, McDaniels, Cliretexan, a limerick, ones where people still live, ones in the south, ones on land, ones in water, new ones, preventive ones, active ones, inactive ones, protocol, dress on Nebraska, tax giving it back, liturgy.

Worthy of love-wrestling with a bear in Alaska, pitter patter, a big section, gigantic books in your face, in the inside of your head.

Won't one person, one tiny little body with it's birdlike voice tell me what they think without looking to someone else, a gibberish without a motive, a hole without a story, without a body moving without them, without them, without the family commercials, the show, the visit, without falling asleep and saying that it's great, without a captive ridiculous polite dinner, without a ridiculous polite laugh, without trial procedures, Parliament.

It wasn't enough. I didn't care. It's a beach, a national seashore, an island, cape, pleasurable, beautiful, physical, full. I didn't want to share this with him. I was cruel and silent. A varied face diffused by love, dreamy watered eyes, cloudlike around the rims. It all comes back to you downtown at night in the city, rapport.

So if the raccoon becomes his house, the taxi driver becomes his job. Memory and the pen move.

How are these people felt? The ones that you talk of and speak of deeply. They are telling me their feelings. I hear them and I like them but I don't feel them coming into me. I don't care. They are translucent. I'm nodding my head and all the time it's reeking of some other form of sympathy. Empathy, the ones who transmit when it's over.

Action, radar technique, characteristic of the fifties, a later version accidents occur. Alexander and the girls, a real gun and does he still work here, an ex-Navy swab, green brachet Marine.

See all of my hearts diffuse, I don't care to leave, my heart is ugly without you. Why do you go out when there is so little left to do?

Exits, I wanted to talk about it, it made sense, it just seemed to slip out. I recognized my voice. I felt guilty, it sounded fake, as if I was falsely enticing someone. It wasn't real or lengthy. I walked toward them and tried to be straightforward. I wanted to look in their eyes. I told him everything and then he announced it. It was true, I missed her. I wanted to breathe them their variations, into myself, I needed that in addition. I wasn't complete. I needed that space below. I was alone again. There was not a single word beside me, it was thousands of eons away, a modified farrah, Italian dinner, funny, lost, temperate, depositions, deposit, maverick, smiling as a child, a man, a secure, soft look in his eye, rat dies and becomes temporary, and knows it. See me in front of the people, in anger seeping through to you, back through the sagging chin, to fight the homogenized zone of time. The child again, slower, thicker, milder, performing the ritual on the mild pick-up, the legendary bus, packing its way up the hill.

Part 9

And he jumped up and down as diligently and dutifully as a fool.

And then he subjugated the baby to this.

I love you and I can't talk to you.

He had nothing of mine and I had nothing of his, just thoughts of the future, quiet lunches in the park, and noisy dinners in foreign languages. He was a door into his own evening. He was religious and kind. He hated ceremony. The people at the party were wrapped in Saran Wrap. I would end this too, an empty ache where two choices were allowed, my empty life, my full life.

I would force schedule, routine, make sense, smile, and disregard. I would practice. It really seems like an apartment tonight, like I'm inside and everything else is outside. Just the way I like it, Lulu Monde.

No more interest in things, ideas, beauty, compassion, reaction, secretions, lesions, emotions, confusion. Had I known you better then? Sounds like he knew what I meant, desireless, make the bed, jump in a big, white marshmallow.

Howdy, midwestern accents are confusing my train of thought. There must be a better way to write this, sharper, something more explicit than sex, something softer than the water in the pool, harder than ice, and something colder than when you leave me hot and lukewarm with your compassion and reassurance that everything is going to be alright. Alright, the Gregorian sunset diminishes in the seventh, as you walk slowly towards the other side of the room. A man for all seasons, responsible and right. Passaic versus Pikesville, calmly smelling the heat.

First I become the victim of myself. I'm lying on top of myself trying to get free. Humorous dogs and it's easy to hide behind the animals and hide behind the she and it. Next I'm on the seventh floor of the Holiday Inn and walking towards my image in the glass. I can break the glass, I don't. Next I'm in the middle chair in the medium water about to save the tall, thin man. At the point he's lying in the bottom of the pool, visibility zero. Next the dream sequence begins, next all of the feelings become monogamous, you who silently react, my only observer, my only friend. The perfectly set table.

The playground is deserted. Sis is making games, a craft she's been doing since last year while Barry lied on the bed surrounding it. I am terrified. It is raining dark and clear. The rain settles my mood. I hear the telephone ring in the distance. Vinny seems to have lost his voice. He calls out various names. Finally I hear my own. Pills are buying necks back into rigid positions.

Next I'm in a hospital that is a long underground tunnel. Next I'm in the displaced apartment, first New York, then Washington. Then I'm on the roof in the west part of town. I'm the movie star. I'm drunk.

A snake who turns into a tall child at night.

An ache in someone else's body, an ache in someone else's house.

When I can't speak of general love, of the failure of love, of the separation of love, of decisive love, a little one in fat suburban skies, a trained seal for your aristocratic friends, the doctor's dilemma.

At once he finds me and I find them. A million monkeys coerce the decision. General directions at noon. Minimum complications tomorrow.

Then it was possessive love, neglected love, strong love, love of someone you have known, love of the temperate zone, of more and more and more and more love, when I walk with my head turned around on my body, my flimsy little music playing, the emotions, hot fun in the summertime, fun in the heat, Hunky Monkey, Joey.

Her hands flutter and she gets out. Short hands, he started out alone and he ended up alone, like the underlying tenseness in casual bars, the elite attitude on the metro, the well dressed patrons, the well dressed computers.

Can you hear me?

Do the book, look at the clock and become the jive turkey, emotional, sexual love, love for the parts of you I love, antiseptic love, child, puppy love.

Since the two days away from the sun, it has become cozy in the room with the tv, the harmonica in the corner and lampshade make it look good. Secure, semi-tough *North Dallas 40*.

It was our generation. Then we talked about it reaching for the kix. You got the courage to visit friends in Virginia, *Glamour, Reflection, Better Nutrition, Essence, Cosmopolitan, Seventeen, Time, Big Deal, Telephone, Tottel's, Miam, Work and Play, Invisible City,* when I leave you sloppily away.

First, feed the cat then sit on the slanted porch and be straight. Secure, then I underestimated the process of the room. Because I want you, too.

Fast love, love that dies, love of money, a love of food, a love of family, family love.

Her ex-love came every day to the pool and brought the pet for her to babysit with as she worked downstairs in the locker room. He would try to be cool. Hey cool, be cool, a big piece of chocolate cake would be for dessert. It all becomes a testimonial to the fact that I hated you when I first met you.

Becomes an invitation becomes protective again becomes general and tough, and white, sorry not white, motorbike, Lynnice.

The king is dead.

The witch is dead.

President dead, summer and it becomes clear again.

I'm driving in a car that crashes into a brick wall. I live. Next I'm at the dance, then the clubhouse, then the drive-in. I take the train station on alone. I travel alone. The water ballerinas have wings on. Next my feet are separated from my body and feet are swimming on the floor; the cats are trying to eat my feet. The noise is excruciating.

I go to the solarium. I'm the star in a Greek tragedy. A black crow is walking on the tops of the buildings of the city, which is a cross between Ocean City and Manhattan. The crow is saying I can't I can't. Monotone. Keeps repeating and becomes a drone. I'm explaining how happy I am in a room with gangsters.

I'm driving out of a very large city. Silhouettes are on each tv screen. They are hanging from the sky. On each screen there is a silhouette of a woman and each woman is waving goodbye.

Love of darkness, masochistic love, love of a lifestyle, self love, self love, self love. Love that is born, boring love. A clothes horse. You can wash it all off with the caress.

A cat keeps stalking around and scabs are dropping off of his body. Peter is reprimanding her. She is laughing. I'm at Friendly's beginning to eat up all of the ice cream. Next I'm at the church with the baby. They don't let me in.

Past love, love for something I can't have, a love life, love of things, love of country.

I'm in an old-fashioned school room and it turns into an elevator. A man is in a bed that is a crib and his mouth is bleeding. I climb into the crib to kiss him.

Fashionable love, a love life. I'm an astronaut trying to understand the HUB factor, love of the unknown practical love, recorded love, love unlimited, left-over love. I'm at Port Authority, then on a platform at sea, then the lockerroom, then trying to locate.

She smiled as if she was everyone's sweetheart. It was enough to make you sick. He was fashionably nervous, at all the proper places. He was humble friendly. She had my books. He had my books. A story in which one read the plot, and described the character. Love of sound, animal love, animalistic love.

First, there was the initiation and then the exaggeration. Air longitude, a smoker's cough, teasing. Solipsism in *Fat City.* Chocolate City. I have some white friends, she says snapping her fingers and then points to her hips which wiggle. She's a spontaneous cleaner. She treats me to a nasty soda. The vegetation—heavy, make-up-heavy, hairstyle and some whites have kinky hair.

Chigra. An assembly, fortitude, Chicago, Armands. Folio the books. List poetry. List accomplishments. Mess with words. Love of words. It was the night we all sat down to play double solitaire. No, it was the night they all decided which poets were which movie stars—Ted-Al, Peter-Clift, rich hippies, friendly kisses, more professional pecks on the cheek. A fresh face, a shrimp.

And now busy with the baby, skinny, work study. There was Johnny, such canary friends, window for window. There was one movie that struck as particularly feminine. Books were trapped.

There was not always love. There was sometimes the emptiness of love (a cab from Drug Fair to work to the hitch up to Skyline Drive). Next the intercom morning announcing stops along the way. Pleasant girls reminiscing of long walks, cat walks, imaginable poetry, lost poetry, imagine poetry.

Sometimes it was the absence of love, of particulars, talk producing nosepainting, as Shakespeare explains it, performance over desire. Sometimes it was the imitation of love, and sometimes it was love, with something missing, with kidding aside.

Tired, study, chicken hands, mirror images, a stone's image, throw it away, and the remarkable fireball, the elementary baptism, the saved wrapper. I see you have it and you really wanted it. Treat yourself good. Trilogy, New Orleans, foxy cannibalism, up and coming Atlanta, Neil. The center becomes slang, becomes a pose of limericks. Just two short legs, a habit, and a pair of legs within.

A lot was read. I don't mean to insult you. Serious classical music and I feel like I can be alone. A stage. He's so convincing you believe he's very real. An overall view, nervous. With, without. An embarrassment of what I want to say using everyone's name that everyone knows and no effect of the twentieth century fifties, sixties, seventies suburbia hum.

Voo-Doo Jewel, and French mulatto beautiful. Jug the one line of sensual persuasion. I have always tried to say it.

Cage an interesting silence. A human mosque. Don't just write about love. Two people in the same room blinded with emotions. The emotions, each securely wrapped. A fault in the computer. Neutro, hungry. Break the boat to bring the boat in. What makes something funny? A weather limerick.

It is difficult to write about fall.The smallest leaf on the uppermost branch had not turned. It was quiet and time passed. Only the Fifth Dimension played in the background. The trip only lasted two days, less than expected. Out in the bay there was just vacant air and the full water. When the sea gulls came down to grab the food, it was as if we had trespassed on their domain. Small boats dotted the sea.

Displaced. A mall, White Flint, New Carolton, Springfield, Belvoir, Landover, and more issues in the city with television as a background. Consistency and repertoire, secure and warm, negligent, and homey, and calculating and successful and practical, exciting, lovely, earnest.

Various times during the day I would daydream on how the reunion would be. Here's where my sense of humor played an important part. But all I kept hearing were apologies.

The only things I could concentrate on the entire day were *Memory* and Mr. Cooper's sincerity. I was enjoying the quiet in the apartment complex. It felt like three years ago when I was living in Alexandria, in the River Towers. Secure, a little displaced and clean. All around me are David's veterinary books. *Anatomy of the Dog, Guide to the Dissection of the Horse, Lameness in Horses, Anatomy of the Dog, Guide to the Dissection of the Horse, Anatomy of the White Rat, The Littlest Cells* and *Animals Without Backbone.* I keep wanting to look through them, but only get to the titles. Concerned equations are muttering past the hallway doors. Art cleans. I wasn't panic stricken or lost. I was so large in the October night, the October morning. I wake up in Lowisetta, Virginia, and wonder what it would have been like to live there before I had to be entertained. A southern, "Oh, honey."

I'm always wondering about the sincerity of my relationships. Each time fall comes, it's New York. I think about the quiet little girl games, the modern use of the English language, calligraphy. If I trace one limerick each day, I'll have a scrapbook, but I won't be a sailor.

The result was the vague sense of aggression on the mess deck. Each little go getter going out to get them. And they do. Everybody wants a piece of the action. I get some too. Vinney and the Night Trippers. If that's your girl, you better have a good time with her because after tonight you're dead.

Tina's sitting on a bench, at the marina, she's depressed like hardly anyone sees her. No reason and a history, the practicing conclusion of religious custom, good intention, and humor. Used as syncopation of a smile. Poor emptiness. He wanted to use the shiny yellow phone, while trying on creams and colognes.

Next, I wrote the letters drawing on my memory. Once there was a man who tried to escape from prison his entire life. Another tried to write coherent paragraphs. He was quiet and tense. I always tried to look at things her way, then I thought of *Stampede,* not in the derogatory sense or the literal sense, but in the sense that I instinctively knew. The laugh became an intricate connection to the mechanism we had formed. Distant, new.

Part 10

Here we are gathering for ourselves, and my whole laugh becomes a shutter, my arm rocketing, my child language will explode, bending repetitions, a choice of events, shallow footprints. My face sits on my other face, my body tries to get out of my other body. My fingers decline.

I like to think he knows me, who I am, false ride, alone, nervous, easygoing, hiding, shadow light coming through the street. Here it is breathing about.

If we really cared deeply, needed them their references, closeness, actions when serious, when joking, and settled it. A large vat growing out of itself.

Feeling these children deep in my throat, dramatizing the event, thinking they know the primitive statue of mother and child, the modern one of the plane, the small cycles in strong events, the failures, and the freedom of thing that cannot live. Pink lights dangle from the trees in the apartment. The voice insures it's talking. Cute! Weather! Chic! Do we connect? Are you with me? Tommy! Concentration! People spitting out shock when it's over. My minds stop me, now, momentarily choosing and popping honey.

Part 11

Inactive ones, ones in the south, ones where the families are allowed, ones where just the men are allowed. The words seeming it drunk (powerless words). When do you think it's an act or when is it real, such as hard life, cynic, boring, funny, lost, sometimes to visit, work, laugh, look at the sound of her voice, watching out, names fall off.

They are talking, passing these windows, envious of the restaurant talks. I'm an interpreter. I interpret ships. Plan, buzz-words.

Crack down, the lima bean's two people and my voice becomes reactive familiar, my voice stares.

I needed that, I wanted to begin while starting to copy. Copying the squeezed pink anchor, he nods approvingly, happy he got a cake this year.

Knowing cooking talking, what to say, snakes are in Alaska, halfwit, poet, your hobby: fucked up poet, think they would care to really understand, the rest only want to eat turkey.

Historic ones, ones that are open to the public, ones that are still standing, the beautiful old ones, the modern ones, the ones that have been redone. Why are the isolated ones? Why are the lonely ones? Why the ones used in the war? Why the ones torn down? Why the falling? The cobblestones, Boston, Virginia, Washington, The Point.

I went there and saw through other eyes, through old eyes, and my body became still. I felt calm and thought cells didn't care, didn't want them, no one in my mind.

But I'm wandering, coming home, father and child, the master of the yes and no, the appearance conversation, credible position, and television, the rented allowance, and actual work, earnest, sweet, bending. They are having fun telling me all the while not to worry that they know you and care for you and your life is only a method to write, like turning it out. I keep seeing scenes, and they are real and dramatic and are corny and are knowing and hospitalized and warranted and lost.

Why the ones we can't find? Why the reunion of the old timers? Their wives look like them.

Ones replaced by technology, ones that are dangerous, ones in a beautiful setting, the first ones, the foolish ones, the ones with their cars and full trucks and families. I should get out here, this is where I want to be not needlessly.

Ones with the winding staircases, ones that are replaced, ones that are referred to in the books, ones that are referred to in the letters, foreign ones, English ones, gray ones, stationary ones.

I've passed here and this is where I've rented my photographer to photograph the subway station for me, in my mind. I haven't done this and in my mind is my future and my legs are walking to take me home, mind thinks home, stop, directing this photographer to a dark Takoma Park where he will photograph the exact angle in the exact sunlight so a beautiful image will show, one of the people ordinarily being herded by their own two feet, and the feet in front of them and behind.

Where are they all exactly? Where are the ones that haven't been built? Where are the ones I'll never know? Where is Frank figuring it? Where is David listening to it? Where is their judgement? Are they judging me, like freedom, like an actual whim, characterized by an easy talker, listener, understanding fondness, encouragement.

Why that look? Where the surprised ones turn into little daggers in the elbowpoint, in the sole of the foot? Where is the man standing on top of Europe?

Look at the encouraging ones, the ones that light the shore, the ones that light internally, the exotic serious ones, the ones who are bent with guilt and apologies, the ones who prepare for the bombs with magazines, the quiet ones, the ones that you need a bridge to get to, the ones with modern conveniences, the old-fashioned picturesque ones, the ones from which the women did the rescues.

This ship is not human. It doesn't live. The land. It is beautiful.

How about when it's quiet and you're feeling right. How about when you know it's right, the elaborations, ready for the trip, pensive, matching, nervous, born. Is the glass on the box real, the wine in it? Birthday, celebrating your birthday. We're so happy you were born, could come and spend these years with us while each wanders about in a large luminous cloud of their own.

Why sometimes, when I look at you, I laugh and complicate my words. I think I'm meaning it. I want to find it. The photograph of the person watching horizontally in a vacant and emptied room. The sound that I give out stops at my center and travels over to you who owns it now. Labor is not of the family or injury.

Lamplights Used to Feed the Deer

EXPLORATION

Time reeked of invitations. You
looked out into stars. They
melted into dark blue bursting.
You could not be sure of such
small details. I knew their ways.
And what each would bring.
And this vastness. How it's all
complete. Mind turning into
mind. It is all a matter of
powerless structures that form
square machines in the name of G-D.
I learned to write it that way.
Other words shall be sacred.
Others should be voiced
quietly. I waited. You waited
for the quiet voice.
    Words on the written page.
It seems the act of waiting and
writing have absolutely nothing
to do with each other—yet each
and everything to do with each
other. It doesn't work because
of two things.

1. Spaces
2. And the interruption
   of things. of walking
   towards the words
   and not thinking of
   coming out of them.
   And of coming home
   to not one thing or
   person, or of familiarity.
   or of this or that but
   of just coming home.
3. Of planning to set out
   this idea or that one.
   of spaces. That seemed
   appropriate. It's the
   way you looked
   walking out into the
   evening meaning as
   much as voices without
   sight. I can see the voice.
   It has no object.
   What I am telling you is
   very clear.

The sound of this song is not right.

We live like fallen rabbits. We
are falling falling. Look away.
The most important things are
lived with eyes closed. everything
everywhere. and hollowed. I
cannot help each day.

Orange in contrast of two colors.

Separateness and Two Spaces
There must be specificity.

Looking to see how much time
has passed and what the clock
said and the urgency with which
one reads the time.
You are approachable. I told
you not to look. You with the
knife caught in your eyelid. Come
over here I have something for
you to do

Change is always. Stepping on ground
How nothing matters and it all matters.
I remember sitting in the room with smoke.
There were either cigarettes or small candles lit and dripping.
They turned into stalactites. There were too many people on the
surface.
They are crowding the edge.

The object is not to get hit.

There is but one truth there is but
one. There is none. References
may be received on request.
Spaces interruptions. Do not let
it affect you; Do not let it have
that impact.
Waiting in darkness. things
began to take form. the
important thing is how at 5 in
the morning I awake only to find
squares on the wall. They had
all separated into separate squares.

The bed is separate.
Why that look on your face?
Why that look? No I don't
waltz through the woods and say
what a beautiful tree the flowers
the green grass, I just walk
through the woods. You think I didn't
hear you. You think I didn't
hear a word you said. I not only
heard the words I heard each
action you made. Every raise of
the eyebrow. Each gesture.
Every wave of the hand, and
instead of piecing them together
It all flowed.

We sat. I heard you breathing.
I don't enjoy the beginnings of
things. If at this quiet darkness
phrases meet. The best is yet to
come. You will not only
disintegrate you will be burned
to death at sundown.
rhythms interrupt us. To have
this want of you. It
has nothing to do with that.
Each and every thing continues.
Look out over that dirt hill.
Each and every thing continuing.

Flash and the dying flowers.
We are living like fallen rabbits
We learn to live
We live

We fall
We have fallen.
We imitate. We have learned to
imitate other animals that crawl
in trees. Your first teacher has
much to do with everything.
The police We are trapped.
The oak tree. The ones
that have been there forever. I
prefer to walk. Words are words
but when you step on leaves you
can hear the noise they make.
What to do with it. What to do.
I smile and remember the exact
space in the room and how we
laughed.
It must have had something to
do with the time of day and not
knowing you. You are not my
friend, you are not my friend.
Breaking off breaking. Shoulders
moved so far ribs show green and
white together.
        And he's not used to your
looks. Tell someone. in the group
how you feel. I remember
pushing two people into tears
and how they flowed.
        Here is my house, the one I
made for you and my family,
and you leave to sleep some
where else and he stays here. Eat
anything you want. We will
measure it tomorrow.

The epitome of the Sky Today.
1. Listening to the man.
2. Her sadness about looking old
3. Her eating habits and wanting everyone to feel good.
4. My brother's success of this material world.
5. Enlightenment.

Lesson One — Have you had experiences?
Yes all kinds of them
Lesson Two — Is there any reason to be upset?
The hot air is right at my face
Lesson Three — Can you drive with me?
I awake earlier anyway.
Lesson Four — I waited.
I fell asleep.
You told me nothing
Lesson Five — It's not a funeral. The branches are always
moving their limbs like long fingers.
Lesson Six — Are you at the farm?
Lesson Seven — The coat
Lesson Eight — Neither matters. We are going to play basket-
ball. Your feet like propellers. You must keep
the window open. Has Daisy May moved in
yet? The girl is very tall. She speaks in small
voices.
Lesson Eight — Head bowed, pensive eyes staring down,
shoulder turned frontward head to side, eyes
wide opened, clenched mouth. eyes holding
the floor, the tears will fall through. I was all
wrong. You charge your moods like the fingers
of a tree.
Lesson Nine — There is no need, there is no need.

Fall through the streets. Objects
have the same effects as sounds.

Humorous to me. Clarity absorbs
every moment. Silence is
awesome. You must feel air move.
You must look forward not back.
It might might return slowly
growing together like the
children's echoes.

More surely: Need to be out of the
Need to be out
Need to be
Need to
Need to
Need.
What the falling off of words can
bring Awareness — positive. Keep
your want. Two blinks mean
yes, one no.
You only want him when there
is a breaking off of, not only of,
words, but of acts and not
peering eyes. You only want when
walking becomes more sporadic.

OLD FASHIONED PEOPLE SITTING ON ROCKS

I am a wallowing wasp. I am a
desperate desert. Cars, riding.
Red flowers inside of the hair
Songs to give: It will give a reason to live
It will give independence.
Street songs — and how the two
words fit together. Before I stop-

ped wanting you. Before the
eyes became terrified. Merge
singing songs of streets be-
fore before. And walking
before the walks were there and
us and you and if I understood
and lost the number and fell
cringing with pain and laughing
you look down and
say, "You are well.
        Your eyes are small."
The need to live   No need to live.
There is a box in the storage
room, Take them — somewhere.

EXTREMITIES. FOUR DEAD:
Foot tapping, arm moving. hand
waving fingers less and less. I
didn't specifically remember
that I had slept that way or that
you had gone into the woods
or Sunday how I will be moving
into a home. It is quite filled
with life. You are chained.
You are free. I am moving. Red
blood in veins. Roads turning.
The door is closed keep your
shoulders back head down.
Spine curved, head down, face
with mine.
Were they eyes or two holes?
So you do have an existence?
Piece by piece.
I will be there until I have to leave.
About sand castles — Empty they fall.

The sandbox is small. Put something in it. From each place — they carried her out in the box. It was just time for her to leave her body. Take off. Fly out.

LOCATIONS

the triangle formed by the bed and dresser and contacts between people The triangle is forming villages. oozing
blisters, infections trying to get out.

The syrup in the town rides people who cannot swim. They kick harder. through their noses, through their ears, through the corners of their eyes. I need to go faster. I have not yet learned to tread water. It is moving me through. Catch it hold it in your hand. The essence was about moving and not moving and the blue vein extending from a point in the wrist down to the fingers.
outside sounds like the ocean. Don't am her anything. She may not understand.

THE FIRE IS BRIGHT AND SO ARE YOUR EYES

There is so much going on without you.
Stars use the night to see. the dandelion field
Stream, falling in getting up the socks
mud and hats and mud turning into ice.
The ballet and lying down and rolling
where is everyone? alone.
Balancing the tree. Turn the stick
to the moon. Sitting with you in the room or not I am tired of
occupation.

The night is long. I watch you turn in your
sleep. The sun was on the railroad. And I looked there was not
    motion
there was not I don't see them running I see
consistencies. You broke the clock. A life
not enough. His hands upward dying.
the sky will shine for you.
It introduced errors. Drift driftwood. About the
facilities of time. When it was too much effort to rise. When it was
eventful to rise. walking each step to drink.
The word changed and you seemed so full your arm on my
    shoulder
your shoulder higher. I was the first to look up

    Maybe it was the vest you
wore or your stature or the
way you move that is always
constant. No moving. or how
you stood at my window and
explained how during the summer
you can watch the sun behind
one building and during the

winter another. You are up
practically each sunrise. then the
Dr. who said—"Don't be afraid
of failure, just do what you have
to do."
    You missed the facts. the
one about how you had to bring
the horses around to the front
of the house and tie them to the
back of the car. The last time I
went I heard all kinds of sounds.
Now I hear quiet chimes. I hear
them with the rain the wet wind.
So far, if he tried for a lifetime to
get near—no time to be near.
Lying down face down. I feel
an obligation to time separate
to space and time and waiting
for the homecoming the noises
are familiar, as the ones I heard
throughout my childhood
voices, keys turning, and laugh-
ing. It does not sound joyous.
Columns and pulled together
and of the
inner and how I would not think
of all of this how it would not
be important.

Do you like animals?

I can appreciate them at a distance.

And how she the girl who said
that appreciates everything at a

distance. Never touching. Never
reaching. Twilight is her favor-
ite time she does not deserve
it She should be locked in the
room at the hour it comes. Waltz
through the trees the cones are
not dead they have only turned.
They are not dead
Look into the mirror You are.
The lights are shut down
By now I had
memorized the department
stores and where each item was
supposed to go.

LISTS

1. The girl that has upset me
2. transitions
3. In flux, Humans worthwhile
4. Time
5. You
6. Caring and not caring
   (Time)
7. Time
8. Time
9. Time
10. Curtains
11. You
12. Final Outcomes.
13. I am trudging through dark bodies
    this time stunted by growths of
    something growing upside down.
    Why must everyone change their
    names. I think of detachment and
    white infectious substances, blood

coming after it. Single files of
people in white robes hooded
walking through Stonehenge.
"we have communicated with
extra terrestial beings."
        You are so good with children.
and anteaters walk like this and
camels and walruses and hippopota-
muses and camels and love birds
and mockingbirds. Sometimes,
I am singing.
                She flies through cotton lunes.

How long will I walk?
How much more?
Where will I be?
If we are only temporary.
Where we are only visitors.

Out of the silence, out of view
What saved you
The Louisiana Purchase. When you sat in the middle of the
floor and
the lights were all out and you the person not writing started to cr
The voices sound like air.

"Why do you like that picture so?
Because the forms that come out.
Why do you like that picture because
the forms come out."

Ginn's Alona
You are safe in large numbers.
The beating in your head is only

representative of what I left
behind for your reading And
what I left behind.
There is no conflict. The bed
awaits your inviting darkness.
Accept
his welcome invitation. Accepts.
Release, release out of light
Knocks on the door. Visitors leave.
I do not wish them to always
leave as I have before. I want
them to stay.
We noticed he started talking about
the judgement day and how he
had to fly and started hanging
around those kind going to the
window and kind of surveying
the area. It was if his attitude
was one of remorse.
        He jumped right before I got
there.
And how this could make me feel
alive. Keeping time occupied and
not even that I keep seeing you
darting in and out of the mountain.
Test this weather
The spring had cleared the path
for falling. I fell into leaves
Someone in the forest picked
me up. I might have been you.
On a dart trip
You scampered over something
half alive
bent down to touch it. It is
breaking

It is alive.
It is dead.
Small. All eyes staring out bulging.
Not being walking in sound
moving of water. making sound.
Remember two things The lake
is always moving. Coldness is
not cruel
The sun rises each morning. All
the competitors. it does not
smile it doesn't wait. it folds.
I am seeing each thing through
holes in the fence. If only I
could lie down and not be expect-
ed to perform. the shadow
under the tree and be straight and
curved at once you would not
have to worry about my inactiv-
ity. That idea you had once
Picking out a person and following him
And how that seems more plausible now
What do you need more The land
or people The activities have end-
ed. Each day has come to an
end. I will need no things.
I am blanketed here. We have
gone too far without you. Forc-
ing each other to be what we are not. Lacking concern.
Giving what?
we are not. number not in
sequence, not in order only
words The names are listed I can stop
hear you sounding them. I would
scratch the trees eyes out if you
would notice that. sound means

more than sight.
She was compact. She was the
kind you would carry in your arms.
She had everything.
And the need for wanting to
get near of arms around and
hands taking the flowers from
cars and of coming home and
presenting the flowers. I was not
only looking I knew they would
be back to lay down with each
other. It was almost inevitable,
that small child the one with her
hair in a pony tail she doesn't
stop running or climbing. Shafts
of light through her hair I will
not go back I will go forward I won't go back.
Look up. Look up You move
too fast. Look up! —
The sky was in motion.
A glass of water Pindar said.
And then I heard the word.
We are landing We are coming
down. You musn't be so cautious
I have waited. You looking not
at me. Your blackness. You spoke
in silence. The spotted hands
and you. The lights
and you.
The stars were the same as the
light below only less and closer.
Hearing the wind. The natives hearing them
believe the soul of a dead animal
goes in a man. Having it all come
together. Trees over the building together.

THREE VOICES LAUGHING IN AIR

1. Help me Help me Help me.
2. I am watching watching.
3. Silence there is no room there is none.
Hole in the center hole before comes deeper
The slips no noise there is only silence that

Leaves me, leaves welling, wailing, falling,
leaves on trees.

PERSONAL ABSTRACTIONS

1. The ice skips until there is no rock no reverse.
2. The rock skips until there is no longer ice because there is very little friction because of fiction surfaces of that because of opposite forces
3. When you swim through water.
Law of Friction of Surfacing of joining together at the end of the day after the activities are over
4. No I do not wish to touch you
because I do not wish to
5. Non commitment — non hurt
6. Non desire
7. You are not drawing towards
8. Who do you love?
9. You followed the sunlight I heard the rustling of clothes I heard the changing forks the saws sawing of not bells of bells of drums
10. I enjoyed trying with you
I do not enjoy listening to people
masticate their food.

Blood oozing out of it's mouth contained tamed. Do not save junk. It breeds unwelcome good-byes in forms of letters. The style stifles your hold on what-ever you hold on to.

Self love, mother love daughter, mother loving daughter, mother loving self, self dies, love lives; daughter living, loving daughter. It wasn't things I was interested in but in kinds of things The day was bright It was difficult to see. And then I stepped inside. The closed eyes and all else was gone. It seemed to end. It was not the music itself but the way it made the portraits come to life. They were not frozen but seemed to take the pose they were frozen into at their making. It was not their exact place but the image with what I was concerned.

How my moving from corner to corner requires attention from you.
Afraid to touch, does not touch Extension the word means reaching out Reaching the shore the falling and upturning sun. People falling through water. The eyes. The gaze turned down. I was sitting in front of the door

it kept opening people out of it.
        To look at something long.
I have walked the country with
you I have not subsided. As
the volcano I am still spitting up.
        Moonlight not included. The
beginning of a very good year.
You were safe. The turning and
upturning of leaves. In these
ideas are concepts mind visual
aids. Fall curving falling falling,
The little girl came out to play
She left no signs no trace
Said I now left the room is dark
The room has left it's place.

Trees spreading The shingles
have split. The boats
have gone home. They have seen
days and are waiting patiently
for evening to come and still
the voices. The setting sun.
The rock bridge. The bridge
Exactly thirty one days. The
trees left partially opened The
dead animals. We went out on
the lake all sparkly gold. We
were keeping very busy without
routines. Almost saved and then
the shoe, the last gasping breath,
and he was gone.

Picture equals picture. they are different

THINGS

Lone dog equal mountain clouds
Railroad tracks equal billboard with wind
Freak equals dead soldier in the wind
The stove equals the light on the bus

DEAD PRESIDENTS: whitened trees corner of birch.
Eyes water, eyes reap water water flowing
water falling   of those qualities
of which you speak so fondly of
        Freedom from self. Blood
water shaking my heart. The
muted greys, the blues, the detail,
the sun crime. I did not shine
today. I was always shining. One
close drop and yours. You moved
slightly and then I followed you
to other numbers. The stillness
convinced me of your
capacity for giving
And the way you moved.
Things do not matter They are
visits from the underworld We
are in a garden each section a
different color the blue ones,
the red ones, and the ones of
orchid,
The snow began to fall. And
then I remembered.
I had been of the flowers.
through which snow had been.
before.
        What were you?

As the trees looked against the
sky, I did not ask how.
If you speak. No I do not wish to
hear the sound of birds they do
not laugh at you. They do not
even know you are alive.
    An ounce of formed light
years formed picture windows

Do not copy type.

The world is ours anyway.
Moulded skin seemed less
vibrant. Each syllable as you
walked through straight. The
word meant something different.
The world did not mean sound.
The doors are locked and down
and down. They did not know
the children ran circles around
the leaves. The closing was not
for them. The air left no trace—
except you.
    When you close your eyes you
can see the micro-organisms. They
are long and irregular in their
patterns. We are going across the
mountain. All falling through, they
are turning upward toward the an-
cient wall.
    And then I looked down. I
saw not only thousands of people
but thousands of people making
noises, wailing. The stores became

the sanctuary. The exchanging of toys and playing with them. The year was sweeter. The beginning of the year. The breeding of human beings into finer specimens of the race. We had gone out for a walk. The night was breathing the daylight They had just begun their marriage. I checked the dialing of the sun and found my answer. I listened. Trains screech under the grey. I found my answer. The days are interims with evenings in between and afterward.

We had been to the fair and looked at the exhibits. We had seen them all before. And all that, the car. What I meant to say was.

The time being too much to bear. I leaving others clothed.

The winter is coming. I am glad.

The trees are escorts. They have learned to see some of us through. They have learned which to take by the hand and which to channel through. They have the breeding of the now silent animals. Time you once said should be worn about the neck and moulded into inconsistencies. I disagreed but was given a necklace. And then I slowly and carefully placed it around my neck.

Bless vacancies They breed welcome invitations. Bless the vessel moving and the rockets turning back. I remembered excretions. I saw you in the parade. You wore four different kinds of masks.

And lacking originality I called them images. You lacked the ability to reinforce. You lacked the ability to watch the pieces fall toward a certain point. You began to walk with your head lifted and suddenly you began to notice things there.

I could never understand why women put dark lines on their eyes. then I looked into the mirror. It is only an exaggeration of life the face said back.

The men in white are wise in their upbringing. They sit and draw pictures. They are foreign to human beings. They are close to pictures. Picture equals picture. Human being equals and my mind comes still, something farther than anything I have known. I read once before we are all in this together. Freeways are not ways of freedom. They cut me.

Dial for joy The naming of

things being temporary. It was
nine thirty. Everything was
closing. The leaves began to
make circles on the cement.
An ounce of two framed hearts
framed this year. The light
framed in two ounces.
one for her moving and one for you.
I remember the time when everyone waited,
The children (Save them
The planes (Save them
The turning chairs — (Save them
the terminals the hallways — (The vines.
And then I remembered — (You,
vines are eternally wrapped
around the sturdier plants) — (You
come out fast with that one.
Unwind them quickly.
Tomorrow's the fun day.
Tomorrow's filled with fun for
the younger ones. We began to
make liquid into streaming colors
and set them down for others
And they did.
  The eyes surrounding terrors.
Trojan heros before you relin-
quished the throne. It was all not
for honor. I was for knowing
the home was base.
  Do you save the coupons?
Could you hold them through
the night? Would the morning
come? Would it come that slowly?
It wasn't that I saw witnesses but
that I was just by. Smiling

mouths are downgrade.

It was the voice. It was the
voices of people I had known
before. It was my own voice. I
wanted to watch you. The
children are cruel. They find
nothing changed. They find
silence.

Yet something increased in
sound. You sat down and for
the first time in your entire life
you listened and heard some-
thing that had nothing to do
with you.

You awaken swollen with passivity.

You're crying out the accusations.
You became the notion of them.

I remember terms made. I
remember tigers and how each
sound was an interruption once
welcomed. And all of this exact-
ness. Each will grow until you
kill it it won't die. Your mouth
hangs off. You can not live for the children.
They are always growing. I went
home that night in splendor. The
rags of ancient creatures swept
across my eyes. The wind
carried you. Each month had a
different animal. We had gone to
see them all. The dramatic ones
cry out (Save me (save me. (I
merely approach you with my
head out of water. I saw the baby
turn blue. I saw you give it life.

You won't find them in the
public schools you won't find
them there. They aren't smiling,
they never smile there. All the
people dressed in white. All the
relaxation. You stood up this
time to watch. Instead they
pressed out your eyes.

The eternal watch. The sheep
wanting to follow one another
and looking to see you. Calming
extractions. You can't find it in
that. I remembered the way to
move and how that felt and how
that was my more vulnerable
period. It wasn't that. It was
your hand reaching mine. It
was that effort of fingers. Your
laugh your voice and the word
they created. Your outside life
was still that prism. What makes
the lines in the sky? What makes
them so bright? We're killing our-
selves. every day. Catfish have long faces.
You can see their insides. The
turtles are flying. They are shoot-
ing up and out into arms and
feet. The rules are my emptiness.
Frost formed inconsistent joy.
I become the witness. Birds over
the school They are flying. I
think of you, organized in your
death, arms folded once more across
the chest. He is running around
the house looking grandeur in

the sun. Do not scorch these new days.

The problem is your counting too much. You're counting the money. You're counting the food. You've even gotten into counting people. Broken windows reek fumes from the bodies. The kids don't smell this. I do not like teaching the ancient order. I like the general thing. I like the fall when it is.

Old skin. I want these arms to wait. I want these arms to wish they were never arms. To grow old with grace. You coming out of the house. What is left is this. You are given X number of children.

My friend makes noise, she listens to those around her. She expects too much. She thinks in generalities. She is tired. She knows what she wants. She knows.

You were not a lady. You travelled too long in trash. A bath could not clean you now. You dried yourself and began to play with ideas. Water seemed the only path.

Nocturnal sense. These creative centuries. The moment where you knew you had nothing to lose. If we didn't have shapes

no arms.
The expulsion of evening and what that brought.
Land, I cried into. The streets were in the sky. Did you stand in river?
Did you cry? Did you see the order? Did you see?
Dominate the air with your surviving factors. Lists of white animals
cursing your world.
The tribe, the tribe, I hear your cry.
learned this through each of the
years of their existence, through
the volcanoes, and their explod-
ing. They have studied hard at
their work. They have escaped
from the fire. It does not touch.
It freezes in their presence. The
children are out from school
There is nothing to do. I see the
enlargements. They are boring.
You keeping your distance. I in
mine, and the vehicles formed by
these. They have set too long to
dry. Kindness was not enough.
I wanted more.

INTRODUCTION

Your explicit introduction of
the world before you were born.
Grotesque arms reach out for
water which is more commonly
known as ice. You born of
liquid. The queen has all the
power. The king must be check-
ed. I looked into your eyes. I

looked into you. The notes dart
in circles around head. Ancient
walls crumble down.
Found eyes. Eyes that were
there.
Eyes that watched. Eyes that
opened and closed opened you.
You thought this an impossibility.
You knew it would never occur.
I believed in found miracles.
Stoned love stoned hate.
stoned writing.
Style does not matter. Colors do.
I heard you stop and scream
Someone someone stop and
listen to me. The leaves are circles
crawling into and out of each
other.
The edge form deep cuts.
We had not decided what to do.
You are coming out of isolation. The
children. It is their birthday.
It is overflowing. Once when you
were up you were always up.
New faces standing in front.
Long faces bodies, quiet and
short. They do not make noise
they flutter about they float in
air. They are not precise in
actions. They are swimming. They
are drowning one tiny boy kick-
ing my leg. You performed this
vague action. The critics raved.
The critics raved. You lost
your hand. The story let go and

before it was the ship exploding
in the soft part of your
brain.
You forgot how to become
and teach the other things.
Walk quietly with other
people and give the assortment
of things. Lamps light the town
offering resistance. Pull down
hard. You will go far.
Glass streets are honest.
Wheat fields lie. Grey skies and
voices merge. What do they do
when they take off the limbs?
Something about distance and the
space created by these and who
wanted to keep it separate and
who wanted to close it and who
didn't know,
and who didn't know.
About suicide and the doctors
unprecedented opinion and excuse
me, excuse me has this ever
happened to you before? Pick up
the flowers there is a note on it.
It may be for you.
America and the use of the
land. cold—heat thirst—drink
every time you were thirsty you drank,
Hunger never entered into it.
These reasons. These incomplete
days. Seasons
filtering through your quivering
fingers. This diversion, skating on ice-this diversion.

There was only one time.
It was this. You were only breath-
ing inside of the tent, surrounded
by air, the apparatus was not in
your nose. You were not ready
for that. Yet I looked at you.
You were the same person but
your eyes were less each day.
I think you knew all along you
were dying.
You are coming up. I am
frightened. What can you do for
three months under water? What
can you do? You had a dream.
The photo machine told you
exactly where to get everything
and how to get it. I saw the last
picture. It fell to the ground
and died. It killed your wife.
You tried to kill it. You ran.
It burned your house.
You fell to your knees. Why
you screamed kneeling. You are
my slave it answered. Cold
pressed steel—against
shoulders. You killed me. You
killed me.
The wind, green grass blow-
ing blowing, fragile ankles and wrists.
Wind that formed chains imprison-
ed us. You go down and come
up somewhere You've never
been.
Smile, all the pleasantries
in that foreign port.

Sticks form miniature men. Is your future in the air? Is your past in the water? Are you walking through doors? Are they walls? He is the ice that is coming through He is the ice melting. The precipitated wrecking. The lost.

Silence breeds a noise so loud and clear only the monarchs are allowed to listen and only they are intelligent to understand. Compassion was the word they used.

The voices come out of the trunks of trees. They come in pairs. They stopped at the bottom and were unsure about going through the roots. The word is difficult you hear one of them say.

1. Hearing
2. Hear and do.
3. Rhymes
4. Parts of the body.
5. Close eyes. Make sounds.

Complete elementary drills. You will come back to these In later years. I can assure you of that.

To be able to move and do the itemized thing. Keys, smelling salts, and the breaking point. That woman – the one up north looks toward the sun. She

travels with a lamplight that she
uses to feed the deer. You look-
ed at her and thought there
were other things to do. I
looked at her. You returned to
the city, made jewels, cloth,
gold bones protruding
from knee caps. The deer are
hungry I answered. Anticipa-
tion seemed old fashioned.
    (Pink lace around the tree.)
You've permeated the building,
You've fallen off. Stoic memor-
ials await the down fall. It is yet
to come. And I remember, and
I remember. The marina is
opened in places I can not see.
It takes courage to talk to you.
You keep shooting arrows
through my head.
    Instead of arrows the next
time you used steel rims of fire.
I am filled. It has shot through
the reach. Where are you?
I have not moved
You can't burn the thing down.
It is always burning.
Have you lit the fire?
Death came by surprise. The fire over the town.
    I have talked to you. You
heard me. I listened to what
you were saying You knew it let
these other creatures go about
the town unknowingly. You
have come home from the belt.

You are just like a child. You know the dinner is not everything. The lights are not either. The problem is that nothing is. Command and watch each step. You could talk about the people you know and all of that or you could look at me straight in the eye and not say a word. and not move and only think about going under water and what other worlds you will find down there

You are foregoing many obstacles and how a letter now and then would not suffice and if this would what kind of human being I would be.

You left your footprints. You left your face. You came back from the desert. I knew you would and suddenly you were not wearing those ridiculous things but looked as I had seen you the first time. Body outstretched. hand holding the head. small poses. I am going home.

Where is that?

Best of this world.

Light on the printed word.

You face the people on the streets. They look at you sideways they look at you straight. They look at you, they try to look through you, they can not

see. You try to be one of the
fish we saw at the aquarium.
The ones you could see through
You fail to cover yourself again.

Black veils cover dangerous
skin. Eyes only show. The pain
this time invisible. You go on a
journey. You do not return.
You do not correspond. One
small cry. and you would come
back for me to torture again and
again. All arms, all limbs, all eyes,
all accepting, you come. You
are with the sun It blocks out
the view and like the spaces in
the rain you used to hide in, you
are hiding again. It is down to
the wood. It is in it It leaves time
for breathing. It leaves time.
Let's play skiis.
We ran around in a circle feet close to the ground.
We went on a train. We rang the bell
We brought this for you. You will love it.
Will you please take off the edge.
I was the only one out there.
There was just the sky, the water,
and the ship. I can see the stars.
They are closer then they have
ever been. They knew you were
crazy. You know nothing. You were crazy and
listened to the music in the air.
It rang out the songs you tried
to sing.

Masticate your food with vengeance.
Hear the bells They use their bodies to ring them. Brass shoes. Where do they lead? The ability to take one thing with time and really take it.

Design with nature. Poses create actuality of last year. You're consuming yourself everyday. Their ancestral name: Rocks. Sheets are forming layers of events from year to year. They complete the old ways for ways of laughter I see your shadow. I see you. I heard half of you saying two things. "Don't think about it And remember the flame is bright and shining." I saw you in the trees sticking out your ridiculous head through the branches trying to disguise yourself as one of the animals Beware of small things. It will cast a shadow. Beware and ask the cactus how it is. Think of it often and talk to it. It requires very little attention. Hesitation and the pauper. He had nothing to lose. The rich kept throwing him money.

Invitation by number.
Glitter on the face. That doesn't

do it. Your smile and the word.
The wilderness and it's element.
The annual rampage. I cried.
You helped me. Both of you
in laughter, one of us in the
circle, backs turned, leaning
towards and away from each
other.
        Moving.
                Where do you live?
                Where do you come from?
                What do you do?
Look on the side
Look over head
Look forward look back look out.

Were you happy?
Did you count leaves on trees?
Did they make you cry?
Did they make you move differently?
Former statues flew away.
The salt melted the rest.
You had your baby in silence.
A woman walks towards herself in the window. She is breaking glass.
        The cleaning of compassionate cries.
        All stood in reverence.
        Your eyes kept leaving the
wind break. You forgot how to
see. The wind howled incessant-
ly. You flew. You ran through
the house. They saw you,
they thought you a bird. You
knew you had been one. Hunt-
ing for unknown components.

In darkness each throbbing grunt.
You ran in circles. You cleaned.
You rearranged. You gave gifts.
You always came back. His laugh-
ter wet and shiny.

It's my move my move my move.
I am frozen.
Run for safety.
Run for your head.
Run for your body
Run for the wind.

GORILLAS

Gorillas are hammering their
brains out. They're climb-
ing out of their cages. Their
motives are not discreet. They
move with agility.
You on the other side of the cage
are frozen. It is black in the morn-
ing You quiver. I tried to tell
you the day I met you. You
denied quietly. You said I was
a lunatic and crouched in the
corner.
    You change your mind today. Shall I break off the leg.
    Shall I hide it?
The monkeys gleaming face. gleaming

The match is about to begin.

Quietly Where are going? What
are you thinking? Voices in the
night. I am walking through the
forest. There are large oak trees
to my right side and all the
creatures that live there on my
left. I walk straight ahead not
looking. You are again hanging
from the left branch on the top
of the field. You are not playing.
You are watching the sun,
its unique era.
    Not having anything to do
with talk or conversation or
what you do or how you do it
or where and when you did this
or accomplished that
and so on.
And then I realized everything,
the thing about all this was
that you are still as a child in
your efforts, and if that is being
childish we should all go back
and walk that way.

Life — please give me time.
Legendary tops of houses. The juxtaposition of it all. What goes on underneath
There is a street to walk on — shiny and hot. Calendars look to the east
The reverend sends messages in Chinese. They are meant to be looked at by others, they are meant to be read by you.

Don't steel rim bars. Don't listen to others. Learn the facts and decide for yourself.

Life and the subsided
vengeance. We were cleaning

the lake. I saw him move. They pronounced each part of his body separately dead. You tried to tell them they were wrong. They would not listen. You bent down, and pressed his heart. and what I knew all along occurred. He turned into one of those beautiful white birds and flew away.

He wasn't smiling but I could tell by the large tear crystallized on his cheek he was completely satisfied. Was this not what he wanted all along? He merely told you lies. He never wanted to be down here in ideas, in body, in mind. He was always somewhere else. If I had known I would have set him free long ago. He just didn't know and I was too selfish to think.

Every year during the fall I go back to the lake where we found his first elements. The water had a strange tint of red to it. There was a sign hitched to the fence that does not allow people to use the water recreational use. Each night I tear it down. Tomorrow evening it is my turn to drown.

Water name meaning water— body meaning water, heart in water, transforming water into waves, and back. Calming all

tension gone It is not an
unpleasant experience. You will
see your entire life pass before
you. You will go with the flow,
An obstruction
may stop you. This is where you
will stay. The first cause is the
land. You will be more than a
number you will be always
changing! Thrashing with the
turn of the earth and moon.

AIR FLIGHT AND THE WRECKAGE

Because of their delicate wavering I am drawn towards.
Unwrapped strength became the answer.
Of the questions you never asked.
Sensibility as a prerequisite caused sanity.
If routine and diversity are synonymous why try to fly?
I wasn't flying I was merely looking down-
trodden individuals take your place on the stage.
The show is yet to begin.
Back home these only came to me in flashes. Not enough to think
out loud only enough to think.
Your spontaneity is born each time you move
One turn of the wrist—I spot it.
One look. It is strong as the hand I hold.

Real people perform mercy kill-
ing every New Years Eve. I
was a victim this year. Tree-
tops are not the highest height.
I saw a tiny bird fly higher.
Debris and forward motion

You are here to stay. You
are absent. You live about me.
You leave, live your own way
form images, speak a lot of
words, do everything, send good-
will, call your parents. You are
a rock falling in love with
separate things of people.
Meet the children They are
waiting for you. They know
how to help. Look, over there,
a whole group, you asked them
to wait. They do. This time
it is dangerous to go alone.
Peace pageants are really
invitations to come out.
Aristocratic lines render after
thoughts. Before your birth
you were merely a person not
freed. You hated everything I
loved. The trees are gifts from
the wilderness. Sanctions
went around the tree. There
was no need for tears there was
only laughter and life and
wanting to plunge deeper and
deeper into the thing.
Your small creation is
making shadows tonight. The
sun makes it possible. Don't
look into other cars. They will
come home in fragments of
glass The woodlands which
occasionally answer back are
having their annual rampage. It

is not a cruel thing. They are
merely trying to reach out to
each other like all of the rest of
us. We are only a bit more
discreet. They sometimes look
at us and strike queer poses
in question or rather in remorse.
They are not swinging like the
kids. They smoulder through
the trunks of trees. They slither
through the roots.

You are in the gymnasium
chasing the ball, in your cos-
tume, in security, at the party,
in blackness, in fatigue, in
desire, in regret, in uniform.

You become an agent for
remorse. You began to care
again You were alive.

Listen, each tiny light
They are shining towards you
they do not turn away
only to Jupiter and her
daughters.

To need the exaggerated space.
January breathing the sun.
Last night the loony birds died. They increased their laughter. They fell in an exaggerated heap. I am warm, I am not afraid to move. I can count the shafts of light on the ceiling. It doesn't matter how many there are. It is thrilling. In the old country you are goodwill. Facts are scientific pictures. The microscope illuminates your so called birth. picture = picture.

MOBILES IN THE ATTIC

I heard every chime. Your
voice comes back to me between
spaces of light. Never I really
heard it. I am ashamed. I can
not sleep. Wind is a beautiful
thing. Hiding its face among
the dead loony birds, it arrives
for the burial. It does not weep
but passes through not knowing.
Flowers on the wall should
never have their hanging but be
allowed to grow into something
unheard of.
Small mouths need feeding.
Come and go out for a pass
You come all out You put
yourself into it. We collected
the candy. I dressed up like a
gypsy. You led the parade in
your rooster mask. The children
went wild with that one. You
are smart you have a lot of
class. You know how to time
things. You know how to take
your time. It lasted long that
day. Everyone came to hear
their fortune. I told them lies.
They never knew it.
Save the Indian's pictures. They may help you later in life.
Stroking the violin, its lucid neck.
Layla means night.
How many days? How many days?
Bridges open and let the boats come through. Walk

towards the wind
Its breaking point is your own. You move with caution.

Wind gaps through
African subculture. What is
she trying to do? Christopher
Columbus has 20/20 vision. He
squints and is moving to New
York. He thinks when school
starts he will be coming back.
He is incorrect.
Not your blackness. not
your white eyes, or stature, not
your teaching or athletic ability.
lights—each in exact rows.
Glass doors leave you to watch
yourself.
Completely   You're finish-
ed with gymnastics each pyra-
mid fell. Lock the doors crash
childishly. Slanted eyes lifted
the sun. Recede in front of
the fire. You fall in.
Heavy with laughter you
exchange gifts. If done correct-
ly. You will see faces of those you do not know.
The issue of organization.
Light years dart about you.
We strike the tamborine and
speak alphabets. You are
worshipping the horse.
Familiar names
visitations. You grow out of
the night as I walk into it,
as the children write their

letters, their not so meager
attempts, their gallant
wanderings, their walking
through the rain, each tiny step.
Bees sleep they make milk
from glands in their head to
quiet the little ones — their line
of motion is straight and direct
wings in motion. They quiet the temperature.
Scientific explorations are
merely explanations for sequins.
They were scattered on your
shoulders today. I glued them
on last night. If we had no
lights, if we were all anonymous,
if we knew what
we were doing. Mandates cried
off the cliff you held.

Canada is green. When
the animals go to sleep for the
winter, I wake up to find
you standing outside my cave —
shoulders slumped. You write
hieroglyphics on the walls. The
plain lands are rising
They navigate their
boats. They always return.
Your political confrontation
and the books not returned.
You are coming out of remains.
Rolling. Golden bridges lifting
you up. Your body soaked,
leaves crept on the ground. The
sound they made.

Four bodies walking on top.
Actual sizes and men who are
really christian. You knew them
all. You knew everyone. Three
types of clouds. Ones that
come before the storm
There will be a day
when we will run out into some-
thing unheard of. We will run
down into other layers of this
earth. We are talking about fly-
ing all of the time. I see more
reason to come down into this
earth. There is so much under-
neath.
        From the bottom of each
cavern stalactites carve the
sides.
        Crust formed generations.
Are we too much in ourselves
to forget this melting of
miracles?
We are writing the epitaphs, we
watched you hang yourself
from a rope from a mountain from a tree. your head hanging
to one side nodding, celestially.
        Hidden brooks-the child-
ren walking on the road. We
will meet you.
After riding, being
filled, after all the unearthly
creatures.
        Because of your darkness
papers were soaked to their
saturation level, laughter

increased, chances not returned.
Walk to the mountain.
Walk to the mountain.
Walk to the top.
Walk through the sky.
Don't try to stop.
Voice alone, voice together with
a voice. Voice with other
sounds. Lights wrapped in
voice. Hysteria. More journeys
into undefined canvases.
We lived in the room for
two weeks only leaving to chop
more wood or go for walks
in the snow.
I knew when
strings. I knew you when you
had been like one of the chick-
ens freshly killed, its head laying
on the ground nervously spurting blood
about until it dropped
one exhausted heap.
It takes time to say now.
I glance at the tracks in the
snow we finally agree on some-
thing.
With these ideas and artistic
pleasures you take to exiles.
It wasn't these things that made
me feel alive.
Alley kids and the silver
gloves. You're all out in front.
In your eyes. The sun coming.
Building human beings. The
sound of a mere voice. Did

you drink the water? Did you
dare to think why?
        I looked into your opening
eyes. Liquid eyes formed pools for your hysteria
You have the power to move.
You have that choice. You lost
it somewhere in freedom. You
can't find the roots.
Fine coats are usually
synonymous with heavy bodies.
Hawaii is the month for Febru-
ary. You're out of water running
on the beach. Water com-
ing up knowing the task.
Always.
        Service men and what it meant to be a man.
        What are you?
        Fortunes that the heat brings.
        Your eyes form smaller skin eyelids.
Walk tall. Lights in the library.
You in transition.
walking the fields waking up each affection.
When they applauded your act.
When you burned.
Fine thread on the flag.
It said tread on me.
You spoke out in front of everyone.
They recorded your message.
Lighter years ahead of you.
Ideas and medicine used either way.
Poetic structure found your wandering hands.

Of this edition, 26 have been lettered A through Z
and signed by the author.